THE GREAT DEPRESSION

The United States in the Thirties

THE GREAT DEPRESSION

The United States in the Thirties

by ROBERT GOLDSTON

ILLUSTRATED

WITH PHOTOGRAPHS

AND DRAWINGS BY DONALD CARRICK

THE BOBBS-MERRILL COMPANY, INC.

INDIANAPOLIS   NEW YORK

PHOTO CREDITS

OPENING PAGES: all photographs are from the Library of Congress
Woman: *Dorothea Lange*
Man and boys: *Arthur Rothstein*
Migrant child: *John Vachon*
Shoes: *Russell Lee*
Farm machinery: *Arthur Rothstein*
Man: *Ben Shahn*
CAVALCADE: following p. 32
Marathon dancers: *UPI*
The F. Scott Fitzgeralds: *UPI*
H. L. Mencken: *UPI*
Al Capone: *UPI*
Darrow, Bryan: *UPI*
Wall Street Crash: *UPI*
Run on Merchant Bank: *UPI*
Bread for hungry miners: *UPI*
Apple sellers: *UPI*
Garment workers riot: *UPI*
Veterans Bonus March: *UPI*
Bonus dug out:
   Underwood & Underwood, L. of C.
MacArthur, Eisenhower: *UPI*
THE FACE OF A NATION: following p. 64
Billboard: *Arthur Rothstein, L. of C.*
"Hoovervilles": *UPI*
Free food dumps: *UPI*
Children at dump:
   Arthur Rothstein, L. of C.
Charleston family:
   Marion Post Wolcott, L. of C.
Men on road: *UPI*
"Hooverville" man:
   Ben Shahn, L. of C.
Working children:
   Arthur Rothstein, L. of C.
Schoolroom: *L. of C.*
Sharecropper family:
   Dorothea Lange, L. of C.
Traveling family: *L. of C.*
Evicted and on the road:

John Vachon, L. of C.
Billboard: *L. of C.*
HEADLINERS: following p. 96
Composite: *L. of C.*
FDR family: *UPI*
Mayor Cermak shot: *UPI*
Blue, Rogers, Cooper, Durante: *UPI*
Dillinger dead: *UPI*
Hauptmann: *UPI*
William Green: *UPI*
Sunflower hat: *UPI*
Dubinsky, LaGuardia, etc.: *UPI*
Rogers, Astaire: *UPI*
Frankensteen, Reuther: *UPI*
Mrs. Roosevelt: *L. of C.*
Armstrong, Sullivan: *UPI*
Justice Hughes and others: *UPI*
Grapes of Wrath cast: *UPI*
THE MARCH OF TIME: following p. 160
NRA poster: *UPI*
Labor comes into its own:
   Carl Mydans, L. of C.
Harry Bridges: *UPI*
San Francisco strikers:
   Dorothea Lange, L. of C.
Depression children:
   Carl Mydans, L. of C.
Rural poverty:
   Arthur Rothstein, L. of C.
Marian Anderson: *UPI*
Rex Theatre:
   Marion Post Wolcott, L. of C.
Hindenburg disaster: *UPI*
Lewis, Wheeler, Townsend: *UPI*
Job lines:
   Marion Post Wolcott, L. of C.
Labor Day spectators:
   Jack Delano, L. of C.
Enlisted for duration: *UPI*
P. 199: *Jack Delano, L. of C.*
Pp. 220-21: *UPI*

THE BOBBS-MERRILL COMPANY, INC.
A Subsidiary of Howard W. Sams & Co., Inc.
Publishers   INDIANAPOLIS   KANSAS CITY   NEW YORK

for Hortense and Roger Hill

Acknowledgments

The author wishes to express his gratitude to:
Harcourt, Brace & World, Inc. for permission to quote from POEMS 1923-1954 by e. e. cummings, © 1954 by e. e. cummings, and from THE PEOPLE YES by Carl Sandburg, © 1936 and 1954 by Carl Sandburg; Holt, Rinehart & Winston, Inc. for permission to quote from "Speech to Those Who Say Comrade" from PUBLIC SPEECH by Archibald MacLeish, © 1936 and 1964 by Archibald MacLeish; Random House, Inc. for permission to quote from "Gold in the North" from THE COLLECTED POETRY OF W. H. AUDEN, © 1954 by W. H. Auden; *The Nation* for permission to quote from "Ella May's Songs" by Margaret Larkin, © October 29, 1929 by *The Nation*; Houghton Mifflin Company for permission to quote from union songs appearing in Arthur Schlesinger, Jr.'s THE COMING OF THE NEW DEAL, © 1959 by Arthur Schlesinger, Jr.; and Mrs. Beatrice Roethke to quote from "The Reckoning" from OPEN HOUSE by Theodore Roethke, © 1941 by Theodore Roethke.

Contents

Photo sections appear following pages 32, 64, 96, and 160.

THE
GREAT
DEPRESSION
The United States in the Thirties

prologue The Two Sides of Paradise

There is only one first-class civilization in the world today. It is right here in the United States.
The Ladies' Home Journal

take it from me kiddo
believe me
my country, 'tis of

you, land of the Cluett
Shirt Boston Garter and Spearmint
Girl With The Wrigley Eyes(of you
land of the Arrow Ide . . .
e. e. cummings

IT WAS Paradise all right—to some, perhaps to most Americans. The decade from 1919 to 1929, the "Roaring Twenties," or the "Gay Twenties," was a period as gaudy, corrupt, vital, vulgar, and, later, romanticized as any in American history. It was a time to enjoy, enjoy, and Americans enjoyed. They delighted in the automobile age, the stock-market age, the motion-picture age, the age of prosperity—all the "ages" which partially defined a ten-year period of American life unlike any that had gone before. While their elders supposedly grew ever richer thanks to Harding Normalcy, Coolidge Prosperity, and Hoover Progress, the young people of the period were popularly believed to divide their time

13

among wild necking sprees in automobiles, wild parties in speak-easies, and wild dances (preferably in scandalously public places such as the steps of the New York Stock Exchange). Their recording angel was F. Scott Fitzgerald, who explained that this was a generation that had "grown up to find all gods dead, all wars fought, all faiths in man shaken." Their symbols were the hip flask, the raccoon coat, short skirts, the Ford roadster, the saxophone, and the dollar sign. Their manner was supposed to be one of gay cynicism, which in turn was meant to mask a deep despair. Those "flaming youth" of the twenties who have survived later depressions, wars, and personal disasters have recalled the era with misty nostalgia, along with the sobering realization that their generation was not, after all, terribly different from others and their behavior no longer considered "scandalous." Yet their America seems a remote, strange land of make-believe to those who never knew it.

It was an America which had withdrawn from world affairs. To most Americans (except the small group of bankers who lent vast sums of money to shaky foreign governments) the rest of the world could go starve, massacre itself, or hang. The Great War fought under the banners of idealism—to make the world safe for democracy—was now seen to have been simply another sordid squabble for trade, gold, and colonies among the European power politicians. Woodrow Wilson's League of Nations (which the United States had refused to join) was viewed as a comic, corrupt, and useless forum for the repetition of empty international slogans. Those who had been part of the great armies "over there" now vaguely felt they had been "suckers," and the mighty American war machine was dismantled, thrown on the scrap heap, and sunk—it would never be needed again.

Domestically, the burning political issue of the decade was not either economic legislation, social reform, or honesty in government. It was whether or not people had a constitutional right to get drunk. With the possible exception of the years following the Civil War, there had never been an era in American history more notable for private greed and public indifference. The twenties were certainly "gay," but with the heavy gaiety of full stomachs and the dizzy gaiety of light heads. Between satisfied bellies and empty minds there was little room left for idealism.

Yet the twenties had promised more. To the men who, under Woodrow Wilson's leadership, guided America through the World War, the peace had promised a chance to remake not only the political but also the social and economic maps of the world. The Industrial Age, now in full flower, had seemed to offer an opportunity to banish poverty, war, and injustice forever. These were the men who had fashioned Woodrow Wilson's program of domestic reform, the New Freedom, and they included men who had inherited the progressive programs of Theodore Roosevelt. Much as these liberals, progressives, and reformers might quarrel over details and programs among themselves, they were united in the belief that America ought to be a country in which human values came before all others. Shortly before his death in 1919 Theodore Roosevelt had declared: "The man who wrongly holds that every human right is secondary to his profit, must now give way to the advocate of human welfare, who rightly maintains that every man holds his property subject to the general right of the community to regulate its use to whatever degree the public welfare may require it." In May, 1919, President Wilson cabled a special message to Congress from Paris (where he was fighting a losing battle to establish a peace based on justice) in which he called for a "new organization of industry," a "genuine democratization of industry," a "cooperation and partnership" between capital and labor. As the hopes of the world seemed, for one brief moment of 1919, to focus on an ideal vision of international peace in Paris, so the hopes of progressive and reform-minded Americans reached a climax at home. But the moment was brief and the hopes were vain. The hard-headed European leaders, Georges Clemenceau of France and Lloyd George of England, sabotaged Wilson's peace proposals in Paris. Later the President's cherished plan for a League of Nations was to be defeated in the American Senate by a group headed by Senator Henry Cabot Lodge. Programs of domestic reform were undermined by a postwar epidemic of "Red-scare" hysteria. And to the defeat of his programs Wilson himself contributed political clumsiness and personal stubbornness.

As America had entered the Great War on a wave of idealism, so it fought through the struggle in a state of hysteria. German agents were seen everywhere, German beer was no longer served, the works of German composers were no longer performed, frankfurters were renamed "victory sausages." Self-appointed 100-per cent Americans made life intolerable for their neighbors of German descent. More significantly, Wilson himself endorsed a policy of ruthless suppression of dissent. Many of the prewar liberals and progressives had opposed America's entry into the conflict because they feared it would undermine democratic ideals at home. When Wilson's government imprisoned the Socialist leader Eugene V. Debs for "sedition" and sent hundreds of pacifists to join him in jail, it seemed that liberal fears were well-grounded. When in 1917 Lenin's Bolsheviks overthrew the tyrannical Czarist government of Russia, American hysteria slowly shifted its focus from the "German menace" to the "Communist menace." Aside from the indisputable fact that Lenin's new government *did* make peace with the common enemy, Germany, some Americans found a "Red scare" quite useful in helping to suppress labor unions and undermine all attempts at social or economic reform. Almost anyone who advocated change could be labeled a Communist.

Wilson's Attorney General, A. Mitchell Palmer, declared in 1920: "Like a prairie-fire, the blaze of revolution was sweeping over every American institution of law and order a year ago. It was eating its way into the homes of the American workman, its sharp tongues of revolutionary heat were licking the altars of churches, leaping into the belfry of the school bell, crawling into the sacred corners of American homes, seeking to replace marriage vows with libertine laws . . ." All this despite the fact that not one American in a thousand knew the difference between a Bolshevik and a Bolshoi ballerina. But Attorney General Palmer (with President Wilson's apparent acceptance) saved America from the supposed dreadful menace by arresting 6,000 people on New Year's Day, 1920. Since no evidence was ever uncovered against any of them, most had to be released later. But those unfortunate enough not to be American citizens were deported as "undesirable aliens." To liberals and progressives it seemed that the worst fears of anti-war spokesmen had now been realized: America had conquered not only Germany but also her own most cherished ideals. Hiram Johnson, the former progressive Governor of California, said in 1920: "The war has set back the people for a generation. They have bowed to a hundred repressive acts. They have become slaves to the government. They are frightened at the excesses in Russia. They are docile; and they will not recover from being so for many years . . . In the end, of course, there will be a revolution, but it will not come in my time."

Perhaps basic to the crumbling of liberal hopes in 1920 was the fact that Americans had been engaged in idealistic crusades for too many years. Beginning in the 1890's there had been William Jennings Bryan's agrarian Populist crusade; in 1898 there had been the somewhat tarnished crusade to deliver Cuba from Spain; after President McKinley's assassination had come the years of Theodore Roosevelt's Progressivism; then, with only a brief pause for the do-nothing administration of President William Howard Taft, had come the crusade for Wilson's New Freedom; this in turn had been swallowed up by the crusade to make the world safe for democracy. By 1920, Americans were tired of crusades. They wanted a return to "normalcy," which each man defined for himself but which generally meant a return to an imaginary period during which men had no need to concern themselves with anything but their own advantage.

In 1920, the Republican candidate for the Presidency, Warren Gamaliel Harding, offered "Return to Normalcy" as his program, and he was elected by a landslide. His vanquished opponents in the election were James M. Cox, Governor of Ohio, and Franklin D. Roosevelt, Wilson's Assistant Secretary of the Navy. Their defeat and Harding's victory ushered in the Roaring Twenties.

Harding was a genial, handsome man who looked like a Presi-

WARREN G. HARDING

dent. Alice Roosevelt Longworth observed of him: "Harding was not a bad man. He was just a slob." Harding dimly realized this. He knew he did not have the qualifications for his high office and sought refuge from the burdens of state in endless poker games, bridge games, stock-market speculations, and the company of political hacks and grafters. To Nicholas Murray Butler, President of Columbia University, Harding admitted: "I am not fit for this office and should never have been here." But his lack of fitness for the Presidency was nothing compared to the low quality of some of his Cabinet members. Attorney General Harry Daugherty divided his time between issuing sweeping injunctions against labor unions (all of whom he labeled Communist) and using the Justice Department to disperse favors and graft to his cronies. Secretary of the Interior Albert B. Fall (who was described by Kansas editor William Allen White as "a cheap, obvious faker") leased the U. S. Naval Oil Reserves at Elk Hills,

California, to Edward L. Doheny in return for a bribe of $100,-
000 in cash. The odor of theft in Harding's administration quickly
became a stench which even the President could not stand. But
he did not have to stand it for long. On August 3, 1923, he died,
a victim of food poisoning or, as some said, suicide or, as others
hinted, murder.

Harding's successor in the White House was Calvin Coolidge,
who, as Governor of Massachusetts in 1919, had used the State
Militia to break up a Boston police strike and won the Republican Vice-Presidential nomination in 1920 on the strength of this
performance. Coolidge was, personally, almost the exact opposite
of Harding. He was silent, reserved, uncongenial, and fanatically
honest. He firmly believed the President governed best who governed least. His personal integrity (and the myth built upon it)
was such that when the Falls-Doheny theft of oil reserves (celebrated as the "Teapot Dome" scandal after the name of one of
the fields in Wyoming) led to Senate investigations and criminal
prosecution, Coolidge was able to ride out the storm, his popularity unimpaired.

Coolidge summed up his views on social and economic issues
in pithy little aphorisms. "The chief business of the American
people," he declared, "is business." And non-interference by
government in the affairs of business summed up his political
philosophy. "The man who builds a factory," he observed,
"builds a temple . . . The man who works there, worships there."
To go on strike was sacrilege. "The law that builds up the people," Coolidge held, "is the law that builds up industry." And
Coolidge dedicated himself to that law which an earlier generation of theorists had labeled *"laissez-faire"* (French, meaning
literally, "let to do," or "leave them alone no matter what"),
which, along with such iron "laws" as that of supply and demand,
high tariffs, the open shop, and government indifference to business practices, summed up the social and economic philosophy
of business and administration leaders. Dedicated to these principles, Coolidge did as little as possible. A White House usher

recalled that no other President ever slept so much. In his *Auto-biography* Coolidge described his golden rule: "It consists in never doing anything that someone else can do for you." He tidied up the mess of corruption he had inherited from Harding, and invited such business and financial titans as Andrew Mellon (who became Secretary of the Treasury) to take over his administration. His popularity was great and he had no trouble at all in winning re-election as President in 1924. In 1925, the magazine *Nation's Business* joyfully observed: "Never before, here or anywhere else, has a government been so completely fused with business."

Coolidge presided over the triumphant reign of prosperity that made the twenties "golden." And this prosperity had very real roots. Although there had been a brief but sharp postwar depression in 1920 and 1921, American industry made a quick recovery. Largely responsible for the industrial boom that followed was the introduction of new products into American life. For example, on the eve of World War I, only half a million automobiles were being produced annually. But during the twenties production reached nearly five million units per year. And the new auto industry created demands on older industries such as rubber, copper, glass, steel, and fabrics. It called for the building of paved roads across the nation and brought about the tremendous expansion of the oil and gasoline refining industries, not to mention the construction of thousands and thousands of gasoline stations which broke out like a rash of measles over the countryside. Basic industries expanded also—coal, steel, machine tools, clothing, and, most dramatically of all, the new electric power industry. For the first time average citizens were buying cars, radios (another new and booming industry), refrigerators, and a host of other new consumer products. The poor seemed to be getting richer, and certainly the rich were getting richer. For the well-to-do, the business civilization of the twenties seemed to promise all that could be expected "this side of Paradise," as F. Scott Fitzgerald titled one of his most popular novels. But Paradise in the twenties had two sides.

CALVIN COOLIDGE

On the far side of Paradise during the golden decade lived the
majority of American farmers and workers. Under the stimulus
of war and postwar demands for food, the American farmer had
increased his yearly output by almost 15 per cent. His crops saved
much of Europe from starvation in 1918 and 1919. But when
European agriculture resumed production, the demand for American food products sharply declined. Farm income in the United
States fell from $17.7 billion in 1919 to $10.5 billion in 1921. The
farm price index fell from 215 to 124 during that same period.
And from this terrific slump American farmers did not recover.
As income shrank, land values dropped. But taxes and mortgage
payments remained the same. As the prices for Midwestern wheat
and Southern cotton tumbled to less than half their wartime
value, American farmers entered a depression which, despite occasional gains, was to last all through the "prosperous" twenties.

Adding social salt to the farmer's economic wounds was his
feeling of being unaccountably "left out" of American life. It

was during the years of World War I and just after that the balance of population in America had shifted from rural to urban. Increasingly, farmers saw their sons and daughters leaving the land for life and work in the cities. And the life they left behind was not simply profitless—it was physically harsh. Despite the boom in electrical power, the private electric utilities companies saw no profit in rural electrification. As a result, the daily drudgery of farm life was not much different in 1925 from what it had been in 1825. And when farmers sought help from the national government, through their Senators, President Coolidge observed: "Farmers have never made money. I don't believe we can do much about it."

In their frustration and growing anger, many farmers turned to older, more primitive views of the world. Thus, during the twenties, the Ku Klux Klan, little more than a memory in the South, saw a rebirth in the Midwest. Klan ritual and Klan hatred of "foreigners" and minorities found a disturbingly wide response among farmers, who vaguely felt that the rest of the country was conspiring to keep them poor. A world-famous example of rural resentment, frustrations, and fear was the Scopes trial in July, 1925. Held in Dayton, Tennessee, the trial of school teacher John T. Scopes on the charge of having taught the theory of evolution to his students brought into dramatic conflict the farmers' old spokesman, William Jennings Bryan (who aided the prosecution), and lawyer Clarence Darrow, who represented sophisticated, scientific, urban America. The verdict went against Scopes in court, but against Bryan and the lingering superstitions of agrarian America, in the minds of thinking men. Ironically, the Republican Party, which had steadfastly opposed aid to farmers, was able to capitalize on rural bitterness when in 1928 it rallied agrarian opposition to the Democratic candidate for the Presidency, Governor Alfred E. Smith of New York, largely on the basis that he was a "city" politician—and a Catholic.

The farmer was not the only guest uninvited to the banquet of prosperity. American labor had also been omitted from the list of invitations. Over thirty million Americans worked for daily or weekly wages during the twenties. And although estimates of the minimum living wage hovered around $2,000 annually, American workers never averaged more than $1,500 per year income during the "golden" decade. The average work week was over fifty hours (longer in some industries). Many steel workers, for example, worked an eighty-four-hour week. Women were paid less than men for equal work, and children were widely employed (especially in the South), at tasks which permanently crippled their growth, for a few cents an hour. The labor union movement concerned itself, under the conservative leadership of the American Federation of Labor, with skilled or semi-skilled craftsmen such as carpenters and plumbers. It did not concern itself with attempting to organize the workers in the new mass-production industries. As a result, membership in labor unions dropped from about 5 million in 1920 to less than 3.5 million in 1929.

Nor did labor unions have many weapons with which to fight for workers' interests. Businessmen could count on the support of state governors in the use of state militia and local police forces to break strikes. The "yellow dog" contract was generally enforced throughout industry. This was a contract signed by prospective employees stating, as a condition of their employment, that they would not join a union. The United States Supreme Court consistently struck down any legislation attempting to better the lot of workers. In 1923 it ruled unconstitutional an attempt to prohibit child labor in the District of Columbia; a year later it voided a law which would have established minimum wages for women and children in the District. Symbolic of the appalling condition of labor during the twenties were the dramatic events which exploded in Gastonia, North Carolina, in the last year of the decade.

Gastonia was a fairly typical Southern textile mill town. Its only industry, the combed-yarn mills, attracted a steady influx of poverty-stricken Carolina backwoods dirt farmers. At the mills they were paid an average $9 per week for sixty-six hours of work. Children of fourteen working in the crowded, dangerous, unsanitary, and steaming mills were paid about $5 a week. The mill workers lived in broken-down shacks owned by the mills and bought their food and clothing on credit at mill-owned stores. Their wages rarely, if ever, were sufficient to pay off their debts for rent and supplies. Early in 1929 labor union organizers appeared in Gastonia. The workers eagerly flocked to their proposed union, and when the mill owners refused to recognize the union, a strike broke out.

Prominent on the union picket lines was Ella May Wiggins, a twenty-nine-year-old mother of nine children who had been working the night shift at one of the mills. When some of her children came down with whooping cough, Ella May asked the mill foreman to put her on the day shift so she could care for her sick babies. The foreman refused and Ella May quit her job. But with no money for medicine she saw four of her children die. From that time on she became a militant in the strike movement. Her songs, with the older melancholy of mountain ballads, helped cheer fellow pickets. When thugs employed by the mill owners beat up union organizers, raided union headquarters, and then turned over union leaders themselves to be arrested by servile local police for "conspiring to revolt," Ella May sang:

> They locked up our leaders, they put them in jail,
> They shoved them in prison, refused to give them bail.
> The workers joined together, and this was their reply:
> We'll never, no, we'll never let our leaders die.

But on September 14, 1929, as Ella May and other workers were riding in the back of an old pick-up truck to a union meeting, local vigilantes, thugs, and sheriff's deputies—all hired or inspired by the mill owners—forced the truck off the road and began shooting into it. Ella May gasped out, "Lord-a-mercy, they done shot and killed me!" At her funeral, as her five remaining children and huddled workers watched a cheap coffin being lowered into the rain-soaked ground, someone added a new couplet to one of Ella May's songs:

> But listen to me, workers,
> A union they do fear;

Let's stand together, workers,
And have a union here.

But not then or there was the principle of unionism to triumph. Nor was it to triumph a few miles away in Marion where police shot and killed seven workers and wounded scores more as the mill owners smashed another attempt to organize. Commenting with heavy sarcasm on the labor agitation (such as it was) in 1925, the President of the National Association of Manufacturers said: "Just listen to the strange philosophies of the *living wage*, the *check-off system*, the *minimum wage, government controlled children* [a reference to child-labor laws], the *closed union shop*, and the *socialistic* redistribution of wealth!" Businessmen, backed by the state and federal governments, protected by the courts, and armed by hired gangsters, were not about to listen.

Yet another group felt themselves outsiders during the twenties. These were the liberals, the intellectuals, the artists, writers, and poets. To them, nothing better symbolized the wholesale destruction of civilized values in the "first-class civilization" than the judicial murder of Nicola Sacco and Bartolomeo Vanzetti, two Italian anarchists arrested in May, 1920, for the killing of a paymaster near Brockton, Massachusetts. Although neither man even knew why he had been arrested, those were the days of Attorney General Palmer's Red scare. The two were found guilty and sentenced to death by a trial judge who boasted of how he had "fixed" "those anarchist bastards." Liberal opinion rallied to the two victims of Massachusetts justice, and, as appeal followed appeal over a period of seven years, the entire world became vitally, almost hysterically, interested in the fate of the two workers. But after seven years of suspense and mounting tension, a final sentence of death was passed against them. On a hot and humid August night, behind the walls of a Boston prison armed as if for a siege, Sacco and Vanzetti were executed. Their last words were: "Our words—our lives—our pains—nothing! The taking of our lives . . . all!" Few people anywhere doubted their innocence. But the first-class civilization demanded sacrifices. Writer Edmund Wilson felt that the execution made liberals "lose their bearings." Poet Edna St. Vincent Millay would ever after see clearly ". . . the ugliness of man, his cruelty, his greed, his lying face." Upton Sinclair felt that the case "killed off the liberals." John Dos Passos cried out, "America our nation has been beaten . . . All right, all right, we are *two* nations."

If so many Americans were alienated from the "golden decade," then just who found the twenties gay? According to the estimates of the Brookings Institution, in the boom year of 1929, 78 per cent of all American families had incomes of less than $3,000. Forty per cent had family incomes of less than $1,500. Only 2.3 per cent of the population enjoyed incomes of over $10,000. Sixty thousand American families, in the highest income brackets, held savings which amounted to the total held by the bottom 25 million families. But it was this minority—and the majority who hoped to become as rich as they—who read the magazine articles, wrote and read the books, created the climate of optimism, and then sold it to the rest of the country. The aim of life was to get rich, and those who were already rich were thought to possess greater talents and virtues and wisdom than those who were not. It was a businessman's world, and the businessman was to be followed.

Perhaps the pinnacle of worship of business (and the depth of vulgarity associated with it) was reached by advertising executive Bruce Barton who in 1925 wrote a best-selling book entitled *The Man Nobody Knows*. The "Man" was Jesus Christ, and Barton celebrated Him as a successful businessman who had "picked up twelve men from the bottom ranks of business, and forged them into an organization that conquered the world." In Barton's world, Henry Ford was a great man. And there is no doubt that the man who put America on wheels and introduced the principles of mass production was, in fact, an industrial genius. But he was also a man who hated Jews, Catholics, foreigners, and intellectuals, despised labor unions, carried a gun, and believed God spoke to him directly. Evidently business ability was no guarantee of general intelligence or even common sense. It was fitting, then, that the twenties found its hero in the "Lone Eagle," Charles A.

Lindbergh, Jr. This daring young man had flown his monoplane from Long Island to Le Bourget field in France. He had done it alone; he had done it because it was there to do; he had done it in a spirit of adventure, not of greed. The wild adulation Lindbergh received when he returned home was perhaps some indication of the deeper yearnings for adventure, decency, and cleanliness which still stirred in American souls in a dirty-handed decade.

But Lindbergh's flight was only a single beacon in the night. The spirit of adventure in America had, during the decade, taken a decidedly ugly turn. When coupled with greed, callousness, and ignorance, it had produced a wave of gangsterism such as the country had never experienced. Basic to the rise of such underworld figures as Al Capone and his mob was the Volstead Act, which became the Eighteenth Amendment to the United States Constitution, forbidding the manufacture or sale of alcoholic beverages within the United States. Passed just after the war, the Volstead Act was a final attempt by a retreating rural America to foist its morals on an urban civilization. It could not be enforced. Americans continued to drink—in "speakeasies" (disguised clubs where liquor was often served in teacups) or at home. Liquor was supplied by home manufacture (bathtub gin) or, more usually, by a new industry, bootlegging (illegal importation of liquor from abroad). Because the entire huge business of supplying drink to America was illegal, the new industry policed itself—with machine guns, grenades, and free and open-handed murder. Local police officials were bribed, local civic leaders winked, and gangsterism suddenly became organized and powerful. With the huge profits derived from bootlegging, gangsters opened new businesses—the numbers racket, prostitution, "protection," and, in a final burst of logic, murder as a business for profit. Everyone else was devoted to the morality of "grab while the grabbing's good," the racketeers felt, so why not they? Nor were their methods very much more ruthless than those of some leading businessmen in other lines of work.

Prosperity promised to go on forever. The management

changed in 1928 when Calvin Coolidge, perhaps with Yankee shrewdness, perhaps because he secretly hoped to be begged, declared, "I do not choose to run for the Presidency." The Republicans promptly nominated Herbert Hoover, who in turn declared that although his administration would be devoted to the interests of business, it would mark a "New Era" in efficiency (Hoover had been an engineer), honesty (he had impeccably administered relief funds during the aftermath of the Great War in Europe), and progress towards some undefined, but surely golden, upland of prosperity where some Americans, at least, would presumably munch through eternity on fields of green dollar bills.

The Democrats nominated Governor Al Smith of New York, a man who had made a progressive and forward-looking governor, but whose appeal was limited in the hinterlands because of his associations with the New York political machine, Tammany Hall, and the fact that he was a Catholic. Despite the fact that Smith enjoyed the support of such liberals as New York's new Governor, Franklin D. Roosevelt, and the surviving Wilsonians, despite the lilt of his campaign song "The Sidewalks of New York," it was a losing battle all the way. The myth of nationwide prosperity was fixed in the national mind. No one could defeat Hoover's "full dinner pail" or "two cars in every garage." Farmers were repelled by Smith's city ways, Southerners by his Catholicism, Negroes because he was a Democrat, and labor support was unorganized and divided.

Herbert Hoover won overwhelmingly on Election Day, 1928. Two months before that November 6th, he said in a campaign speech: "We in America today are nearer to the final triumph over poverty than ever before in the history of any land. The poorhouse is vanishing from among us. We have not yet reached the goal, but, given a chance to go forward with the policies of the last eight years, we shall soon with the help of God be in sight of the day when poverty will be banished from this nation." Mr. Hoover had perhaps never heard of *hubris*, a Greek word describing defiance of the gods or, more colloquially, "Pride goeth before a fall."

one The Crash

The Jazz Age now raced along under its own power,
served by great filling stations full of money . . .
Even when you were broke you didn't worry about money,
because it was in such profusion around you.
F. Scott Fitzgerald

All people are most credulous when they are most happy.
Walter Bagehot

THE FILLING stations were never fuller than on September 3,
1929. On that day the New York Stock Exchange hit a new all-
time high; the prices of corporate stocks listed on the Exchange,
expressed in point values, reached dizzy pinnacles of speculative
value. Thus a share of American Telephone was worth 304 points
(dollars); General Electric, 396; New York Central was quoted
at 256; United States Steel at 261; Radio Corporation at 505; and
other stocks—both listed and unlisted on the Exchange—reached
similar heights. Nor were these stock quotations of interest only
to brokers or financiers; in 1929 over one and a half million Americans had invested part or all of their savings in stocks. "Playing
the market" had become, during the preceding few years, a national sport which rivaled baseball in popularity. Chauffeurs and
window cleaners, housewives and wrestlers, farmers, diplomats,
clerks, and shoeshine boys—every type and kind of American
seemed infected with an obsession to play the Stock Market
Game.

The classical theory of the stock market was easy enough to comprehend. An industrialist, or a corporation, required money to establish plants or to enlarge existing facilities or to renew machine tools. Instead of trying to borrow the relatively large sums involved from a bank, the corporation sold, to anyone with the means to buy, a share of stock—a glorified form of I.O.U. As they would to a bank, the corporation paid interest on the money loaned to the person who had bought the share of stock. The interest payments, paid quarterly or semi-annually, were known as dividends. Unlike interest payments to a bank, however, the value of the dividend rose or fell in relation to the success—or lack of it—of the enterprise involved. Thus, an individual with surplus savings had a chance to put those savings to work earning larger (generally) rates of interest than he would have received from a bank or from government bonds, for instance. The corporation got its money for expansion, and everyone was happy—except those, of course, who foolishly invested their money in corporations whose business declined and who could therefore pay no dividends. Corporations issued two kinds of stock: common stock and preferred stock. Purchase of common stock might bring financial rewards, but it brought no voice in the management of the corporation. Purchase of preferred stock carried with it the right to vote on corporation policies, the voting power being in proportion to the amount of preferred stock owned. Of course, industrialists and corporate managers tried to make sure that at least 51 per cent of the preferred stock remained in their own hands so that no coalition of stockholders could grab control of the corporation from them, or dictate its policies.

But there was, of course, another aspect to stock ownership. As corporate business expanded or declined, the value of the shares of stock offered for sale rose or fell on the Stock Exchange, which was no more than a convenient place for people to buy and sell stocks. Thus, if General Electric, for example, announced that last year's business had been much better than that of the year before (and therefore profits distributed in the form of dividends would be higher), the value of a share of its stock would go up. Some people bought stocks not so much for the dividends that they might pay as for the fact that their value would rise and they could be sold at a profit. This was known as speculation, rather than investment. And from 1927 to 1929, the fever of speculation seemed to have gripped the country.

In 1929 the rules of the Stock Market Game were admirably contrived to encourage speculation. If you wanted to get rich quick, without working, all you had to do was to get in touch with one of the many New York brokerage houses (a broker was a man who bought and sold stocks on the Exchange on behalf of investors or speculators) which had offices in most cities and towns from coast to coast. You asked them to buy as many shares of stock in as likely looking a corporation as you could afford. You did not have to pay the full value of the stocks; you could buy them "on margin," which meant that you had only to put up (in 1929) about 40 per cent of the face value of the stock. The broker would supply the rest on credit. If, for example, you wanted to buy a share of stock which cost $100, you paid your broker $40 in cash. He put up the other $60. Then you sat back and waited for the price of the stock to rise. If it rose to, say, $200 per share you could sell it, pay the broker his $60, recover your original $40, and make $100 in profit. The brokers got the money to put up for their share of margin holdings from the banks, at stiff interest rates, to be sure. Of course, if by some mischance the value of your $100 share declined—say, to $50—then the broker (who was holding your stock as his only security against default on repayment of his $60) might send you a "margin call." This meant you had to send him more cash if you wanted to hang onto the stock. For, if your share was now worth only $50 and the broker sold it in an attempt to get back his $60, he would take a $10 loss. So he might well send you a demand for $10 more cash to preserve your speculative investment. If you did not come up with the cash, he could sell your stock, taking a $10 loss himself while you took a $40 loss.

It can be easily seen that much depended on confidence. You

had to be confident that stock values would, in fact, rise. Your broker had to be confident, too. Therefore a high premium was put on statements by bankers, financiers, Stock Exchange personnel, and other money wizards as to the health of the stock market. When such men as Richard Whitney, a broker for the banking house of J. P. Morgan (and Vice President of the Exchange), or Charles Mitchell of the National City Bank, or John D. Rockefeller (who almost never speculated in stocks) declared that business prospects were bright, stock values rose. When, on occasion, critics proclaimed business prospects poor or muttered that stock prices were inflated, they were denounced not only as fools but as enemies of prosperity, since such remarks could only shake public confidence in the market and lead to a lowering of stock prices.

But the essence of the stock market boom of the late twenties was speculative. Stock prices did not reflect real values. They did not reflect the worth of the industrial plant of a company, or the value of its products, or even the size of the dividends it paid on its stock. They reflected instead the hunches and guesses of speculators as to what tomorrow's demand might be for stock from people who, in turn, were speculating. A man owned a share of General Electric stock because he was confident that very soon another man would pay him more money for it than he had paid. And that other man bought it for the same reason. And from 1926 to 1929, aside from occasional "wobbles" in the prices of stocks, their value rose in a dizzy spiral of speculative buying. Everybody was sure to get rich.

In fact, not getting rich was regarded as a sign of willful stubbornness or stupidity. In an article written for *The Ladies' Home Journal*, John J. Raskob, a respected financier and Chairman of the Democratic National Committee, discovered that any worker who saved $15 per month, invested it in sound common stocks, and reinvested his dividends in those same stocks would, in twenty years, be worth $80,000. Mr. Raskob's article was aggressively entitled "Everybody Ought to Be Rich!"

cavalcade

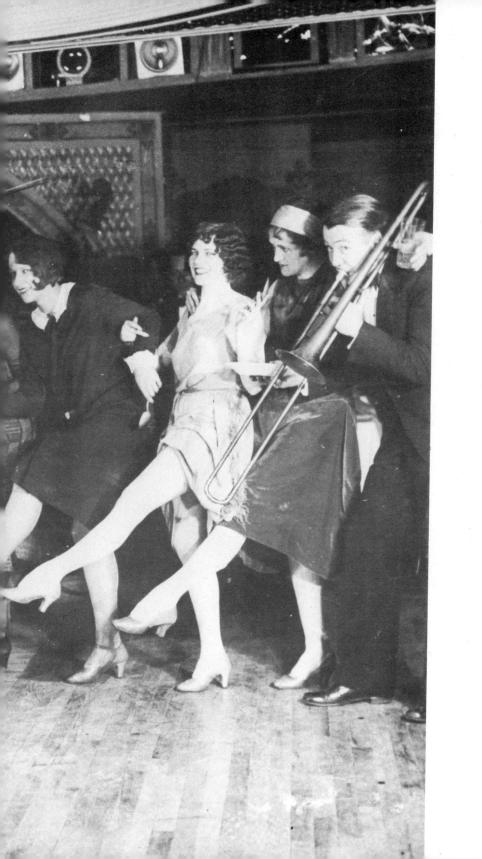

The gas stations were still pumping money on this side of paradise, and Scott and Zelda Fitzgerald reveled in what America produced best—*things*.

Not all Americans were happy about it. H. L. Mencken described American society as "pointless," "witless," "idiotic." Presidents were "baboons," Senators "thieves, morons and swine," and civilization something alien to the American dream.

Al Capone (center), on the other hand, would have simply shrugged and repeated P. T. Barnum's classic crack: "There's one born every minute." Al had his own means of getting *things*—and they were only a little rougher than some business practices of the times. He, too, partook of the American dream.

Not that idealism was completely dead. Clarence Darrow (left) and
William Jennings Bryan (right) met in a steaming courtroom in Tennessee to argue ideals—and Bryan's rural fundamentalism suffered a
mortal blow as urbanity and sophistication began to replace backwoods
religiosity in American life. The American dream was changing.

Then, on Black Thursday, the American dream turned into a nightmare as Wall Street's Stock Market Boom turned into The Crash. People were stunned, unbelieving at first. Paper fortunes had vanished, but money was the foundation of American life. Disbelief turned to panic as people besieged the banks (this one was in New Jersey) trying to withdraw their life's savings—often too late. The banks began to collapse and industrial production ground to a halt.

Men lost their jobs, then their savings, then their credit—and finally their pride and hope. Here they lined up humbly in Pennsylvania to receive the bread of charity while business and political leaders assured them that prosperity was just around the corner.

But around the corner in most American cities were apple sellers. You could pay a nickel or a dollar for the apples—it didn't matter. It was thinly disguised begging, and the fruit was bitter.

When it became too bitter, workers and unemployed alike tried to organize to enforce union standards on industry. But as these lady garment workers found out, industry had its own private armies of thugs (here displaying their courage by beating up a woman) who were generally supported by local police and the courts.

Perhaps the answer was in Washington. Thousands of World War I veterans thought so. From every corner of the country they converged on the nation's capital—not just to win their promised veterans' bonus, but to try to awaken Congress and the President to the country's needs.

They were peaceful enough in their tar-paper shanties; proud of their comradeship, still clinging to faith in democratic processes, waiting for help from a government determined not to give it. Instead of help they received tear gas, bayonet jabs and fire as they were run out of their capital.

When it was all over, Chief-of-Staff General Douglas MacArthur (being watched by his junior officer, Major Dwight D. Eisenhower) wiped his face and remarked that he'd liberated more than one city from enemy occupation in his time. It seemed that the American people had become the enemy.

But despite the one and a half million Americans who played the market in 1929 most stocks, and practically all preferred stocks, were owned by the rich or by companies set up for the purpose of stockholding. It seemed one could make easy money so fast on the market that many corporations, instead of using the money received for their stocks for plant expansion or renewal or other industrial purposes, took the money and reinvested it in turn in other stocks. As companies were organized for the sole purpose of holding stock in other companies, the corporate struc ture became exceedingly intricate. In fact, in later years Samuel Insull, the great Chicago financial wizard (and, as it turned out, thief), admitted that his own companies were so extensive and complicated that even he did not understand his own organization. Thus, if anything went wrong, fewer and fewer people would be able to predict where the chips might fall, or whose chips they would be.

A new way to play the market was also invented during the late twenties. This was the formation of "investment trusts." These corporations would invest your money for you. They were supposedly staffed by stock market experts who could cannily predict the rise and fall of stocks and who had, besides, "inside tips" about stock values. Therefore they could make more money with your money than you could. Obviously, the officers and staff of the investment trust had to be paid for their services, so no matter what happened their customers lost part of their money to begin with. And to add a final complication to everything, the investment trusts in turn sold their own stock on the market. Furthermore, the sale of stock was largely uncontrolled in 1929. The Stock Exchange, a private institution, was self-policing in regard to the honesty of its members. But self-policing turned out to be a weak reed upon which to lean. Stocks were offered for sale by an advertising prospectus, and the prospectus often lied. It might describe in glowing terms a gold mining company which was later discovered to own not a single pick or shovel. But it didn't matter —confidence was the thing. And confidence arose from the uncontrolled optimism of a supposedly prosperous decade, and from the simple-minded greed which had become the central meaning of American life.

There were some means of control. Primary among them was the Federal Reserve System discount rate which could be raised or lowered by the government-appointed members of the Federal Reserve Board. This is not a complicated procedure to understand. Banks throughout the country were loaning money to brokers so that they could put up their 60 per cent of the value of stocks bought on margin. In return the banks received high interest rates on this money (in 1929, 12 per cent). But in order to get the money to lend, the banks had often to turn to the Federal Reserve System banks, operated under government regulation. If the Federal Reserve Banks increased the interest rate they demanded in order to lend money to private banks, then those private banks in turn would have to increase the interest rates they charged the brokers. If interest rates were low, then bank lending money was cheap and easy to come by, and if interest rates were high many brokers would not be able to afford to borrow, and their stock-buying would diminish. But if the Federal Reserve Banks increased their interest rates, then local banks would have to increase their interest rates for loans to farmers, homeowners, and businessmen as well as brokers. Thus business activity would shrivel, presumably, and the very depression the Federal Reserve had sought to avoid might be initiated. Furthermore, any announcement that the Federal Reserve Board was raising its interest rates would imply that it thought too much money was being poured into the stock market, that stock values were inflated. This in turn might cause a collapse of confidence. People might start selling their stocks, and the entire complex and tipsy structure might topple.

Government taxes were not, in 1929, a means of control—either direct or indirect. Income taxes were extremely low (and extremely easy to evade on the part of the rich); there was no such thing as a corporation excess-profits tax, and only a token inheritance tax. Thus the government could not remove speculative money from circulation by raising taxes (if it had tried to impose new ones the conservative Supreme Court would have declared them unconstitutional). Furthermore, Republican tax policy was largely dictated by Andrew Mellon, Secretary of the Treasury under Coolidge and under Hoover, too. Mellon, who had made a large fortune in banking, had stated: "The Government is just a business, and can and should be run on business principles." His first proclaimed interest was to balance the budget. But he evidently had a greater interest—the reduction of income taxes for the rich and for himself personally. A man who earned $1 million a year in 1929 (and was stupid enough not to disguise his income through the many possible devices dreamed up by tax lawyers) would have to pay almost $300,000 in taxes (today he'd pay more than $900,000). Mellon argued that such tax rates were confiscatory, and through the years of his control of the Treasury he steadily chipped away at the higher-bracket taxes. Moreover, he made it a policy to secretly refund taxes to individuals and corporations through various loop-holes in the law. During the Coolidge administration he refunded no less than $3.5 billion in this way. Millions of dollars, it later turned out, were refunded to corporations owned by Mr. Mellon himself, especially to the Gulf Oil Company. Furthermore, to make certain that he paid the lowest possible personal income tax, the Secretary of the Treasury had the Commissioner of Internal Revenue submit a memorandum to him listing ten possible ways of avoiding income tax, and send over a government tax expert who personally prepared Mellon's income tax to be certain he paid next to nothing. Needless to say, Andrew Mellon also speculated, and heavily, in the stock market. "A decrease in taxes," he declared, "causes an inspiration to trade and commerce"— and leaves more money to be injected into the stock market boom, he might have added.

While bankers were busily pumping cash into brokerage houses at 12 per cent interest, they were also pumping money into foreign governments by means of buying those governments' bonds. This, too, reflected government policy. Republicans, as the party of industry since 1870, had always favored high tariffs. When the United States was developing its industrial plant, it seemed important and logical to protect infant industries from massive foreign competition by imposing high customs duties on foreign products imported into the United States. This made them more expensive—and therefore less attractive to buyers. The Democrats, on the other hand, had often urged lower tariffs on behalf of the farmers who had to buy manufactured articles. Woodrow Wilson brought forward a new reason for low tariffs: the United States by 1900 was already tremendously developed industrially. The problem was no longer to protect American industry but to find it foreign export markets. But foreign countries could not buy American goods if they had no dollars with which to buy them. And Wilson thought the only way they could accumulate dollars was by selling their own products in the United States. So foreign trade became a two-way street. High tariffs at home would mean high tariffs abroad, and American exports would suffer. But Wilson had overlooked one possible way that foreign governments could get dollars to buy American goods, even if they could not sell their products in the United States. This was by way of borrowing the dollars from American bankers. Herbert Hoover, while he was Secretary of Commerce under Harding and Coolidge and also later when he won the Presidency himself, encouraged high tariffs and massive foreign loans. What would happen if such nations as, for example, Germany or England or Peru should suffer an economic collapse and then not be able to repay these loans remained beyond the realm of government speculation. Billions and billions of American dollars flowed abroad during the twenties in the form of loans to governments or to foreign business enterprises.

Part of this money, at least, returned to the United States, not so much in the purchase of American exports as in foreign bankers' investments in the stock market. Bank loans to brokers in New York were earning 12 per cent, and that terrific interest rate encouraged bankers throughout the world to pump money into the same lucrative market. An indication of how fast bank loans to brokers expanded (domestic as well as foreign) was the fact that although such loans totaled $1.5 billion in 1923, by 1929 they had risen to $6 billion! This meant that nearly six times as much stock was being held on margin in 1929 as in 1923, which was a fairly good index of the rise in speculation as opposed to investment.

While the stock market continued its joyous spiral upward, certain danger signs began to appear during the summer of 1929. The construction industry, always a barometer of general business weather, showed a decline of over $1 billion between 1928 and 1929. Industrial production, which reached a peak in July, 1929, started to decline in August, and so did employment. Business inventories—that is, reserve stocks of unsold goods—rose from $500 million in 1928 to over $1.8 billion in 1929. The index figure for the rate of consumer purchasing fell from 7.4 per cent in 1927–1928 to a meager 1.5 per cent in 1929. Aware of these trends, and influenced by the very few voices raised in alarm at the boom, the Federal Reserve Board advised banks throughout the country that they ought not to lend money for speculative purposes. When this warning was ignored, the board raised the discount rate on loans to private banks to 6 per cent in August, 1929. But this still left so heavy a margin of profit to banks lending money at 12 per cent that it had little effect in drying up the flood of gold into the stock market.

Behind these statistics there lay an even deeper maladjustment of the American economy. With the introduction of mass production techniques and new machines, the output per worker in American industry rose during the twenties by over 40 per cent. But the wages earned by American workers rose only 7 per cent. The resultant savings were not passed along to the public. According to classical economic theory, an increase in the efficiency of production should have led to a lowering of prices as corporations competed for the market. But corporations were not competing for the market. They had grown so large, their interdependence both indirect and (through complicated holding companies) direct had grown so great, that they "fixed" prices. This was illegal according to the terms of the Sherman Anti-Trust Law, but both Coolidge and Hoover regarded that law as an impediment to industrial development and refused to enforce it. Thus, as workers' efficiency increased and industrial production soared, corporations skimmed off the resulting gains as direct profits. And these profits were more and more used to speculate in the stock market. By not passing their new savings on to workers in either increased wages or much lower prices, industry was constricting its own market. But it began to seem less and less important how many products were sold—money was to be made not by production and work, but by stock speculation.

The stock market suffered a few mild tremors in stock prices during September, 1929. These fluctuations were soon smoothed out and brokers confidently awaited a new rise in stock prices. But October brought wilder fluctuations. Then, on Thursday, October 24, 1929 (to be known ever afterwards as "Black Thursday"), the stock market speculation came down with an awful crash. Suddenly it seemed that nobody had any more confidence in rising stock prices. Everyone wanted to sell at once. Prices fell drastically. That day nearly 13 million shares of stock were traded —at lower and lower prices (some of them could find no buyers at any price). The floor of the New York Stock Exchange became a scene of wild scrambling, desperate shouting as brokers frantically rushed to unload their stocks before prices fell even further. A very real, personal, panic seized not only the Exchange but also the crowds that began to accumulate outside its doors. Spotting a workman atop one of the tall Wall Street buildings, the crowd assumed he was a broker preparing to jump and called the police. At noon the scene in the Exchange was so hysterical that officials closed the visitors' gallery (putting out an English visitor, Winston Churchill).

But even as visitors were being ushered from the Exchange, calm was being brought to the floor. At noon the news was spread that a meeting of important bankers and financiers was taking place at 23 Wall Street, the offices of J. P. Morgan and Company. There were gathered Charles Mitchell, representing the National City Bank, William C. Potter of the Guaranty Trust Company, Albert H. Wiggin from the Chase National Bank, Seward

Prosser of the Bankers Trust Company, and Thomas W. Lamont, a Morgan partner. These gentlemen had decided that the time had come to organize support for the market. They would pool their financial resources (to the tune of $40 million each) to buy stocks at reasonable prices. This, they thought, would put an end to selling. Furthermore, the very fact that such financial wizards were confident enough to make heavy stock purchases ought to put an end to panic sales. Their assumptions were correct. When news of the meeting reached the Exchange, prices immediately steadied. Then Richard Whitney appeared, made his way through the milling crowd of stock brokers and offered to buy steel stocks at 205, although they were now quoted at 193. Immediately fear vanished and prices began to rise—in the Exchange.

But, unfortunately, not all the selling was being done in the Exchange. Much of it was ordered by fearful clients watching ticker-tape machines across the country. And because of the heavy volume of business, the ticker-tapes were running one to two hours behind prices and events in the Exchange itself. Selling orders continued to pour in from San Francisco, Albuquerque, Miami, Chicago, Des Moines. Nevertheless, as the day ended, although stocks had taken a terrific tumble, things looked better. Prices remained fairly stable during Friday and Saturday.

Over the weekend, businessmen vied with each other making reassuring statements about the market. A Boston investment trust took a large ad in the *Wall Street Journal* which cried, "S-T-E-A-D-Y Everybody! Calm thinking is in order. Heed the words of America's greatest bankers!" But while the Exchange was closed on Sunday, Americans throughout the nation had time to think over their prospects. The results of their thoughts were pessimistic. On Monday when the market reopened, although trading was less, prices fell more drastically even than on Thursday. And despite the fact that the bankers once again assembled in the offices of Morgan and Company, on this day there was no recovery. It was apparent, indeed, that the bankers would not again come to the rescue of the market. Tuesday,

October 29, turned out to be the worst day in the 112-year history of the New York Stock Exchange. More than 16 million shares of stock changed hands; the ticker-tape ran two hours behind in reporting the plummeting prices. Many stocks lost more than half their value. And news rapidly spread that the bankers, far from trying fruitlessly to stabilize the market, were now desperately selling their own stocks, trying to get out before they were utterly wiped out.

The speculative boom had been built like an upside-down pyramid, based on borrowed money. Now it collapsed like an upside-down pyramid. Stock brokers, heavily in debt to the banks for the money they had put up to hold their clients' stocks, were frantically sending out margin calls to thousands and thousands of people throughout the country. Because the stocks had declined in value to and past the point where their sale would at least enable a broker to break even and pay his debt to the banks, the brokers were demanding that their customers put up more money, or have their stocks sold for whatever they would bring. But very many people had no more cash to send. Their stocks were sold, which drove prices down still further. It was not only the small individual customers who could not afford to hang onto their stocks; the investment trusts were also going broke. The large investment trust of Goldman, Sachs Inc., for example, saw its stock fall from near 100 to 3 points in two days. All the corporations and banks which had invested in the market were losing even more heavily than individuals. Then, when banks which had lent money to brokers demanded repayment, broker after broker had to default. Just as stock prices had spiraled upwards, they now spiraled down—but at an infinitely faster pace.

Public statements by leading financiers and businessmen now had no more effect on the determination of investors to get out of the market. John D. Rockefeller was prevailed upon to declare, for instance: "Believing that fundamental conditions of the country are sound . . . my son and I have for some days been purchasing sound common stocks." Eddie Cantor, the comedian, commented, "Sure, who else had any money left?" Nerves were so raw in the financial districts that when on Thursday, October 31, a little boy exploded some firecrackers on La Salle Street in Chicago, rumors quickly spread that gangsters who had lost heavily on the market were out shooting up the street. Squad cars of police arrived to find a very bewildered little boy.

The New York Stock Exchange was closed that Thursday afternoon and did not reopen until the following Monday. This was primarily to give stock brokers and their harried clerks a chance to catch up with the immense amount of paper work that went into recording the disaster. It was also hoped that the closing would give the nation a chance to calm down. But it had the opposite effect. During the following week stock prices slumped still lower. It was during these dreary days that the legend grew that stock brokers and bankers were hurling themselves from high windows and that a wave of suicide was sweeping over the speculators. Actually this was untrue. Despite the fact that there is a cherished legend in American folklore that pedestrians on Wall Street had to scurry out of the way of falling financiers, no such wave of suicides took place. Those (and they were countless) whose life savings had been wiped out were far too stunned and depressed to think of anything so violent as suicide. The show business newspaper, *Variety*, summed it up in an immortal head-line on October 30: "WALL STREET LAYS AN EGG." By mid-November, the stock market had suffered an average 40 per cent loss in values—a loss that represented, on paper at least, $26 billion! During the following months and years the market would sink even further.

The collapse of the stock market produced a chain reaction throughout the American economy. Most of the buying power of the country was, as we have seen, concentrated in the hands of a minority of rich people. And these were the very people whose bank accounts had been wiped out. Consumer spending went into a sudden and pronounced decline, beginning especially with luxury items. Because of the fact that industry had not shared its profits with labor in the form of increased wages for increased productivity, there was no great reservoir of mass purchasing power to keep goods moving. And in light of the disaster, department stores and other businesses whose inventories were, it will be recalled, especially heavy in 1929, slowed down or stopped altogether their orders from manufacturers. Industry in turn felt compelled to cut back production, and this meant firing employees. Because businessmen had so successfully and savagely fought the idea of labor unions, there was no organized way for workers to save their jobs. And out-of-work people did not make good customers. To add to the catastrophe, many corporations which had speculated in the stock market had suffered losses so severe that they were forced into bankruptcy, thereby throwing additional masses of employees out of work. Other companies which had been incorporated into complex financial empires through holding companies and other devices collapsed, even though their production and business prospects were not endangered; they collapsed as part of those falling empires. Banks which had lent huge sums to brokers, and had, in some cases, speculated directly in the market, now worried whether they could raise enough cash to pay back their individual depositors, should those depositors seek to draw their savings out of the bank. And those heavy loans to foreign governments and industries were now in grave danger. Because foreign financiers had themselves plunged so heavily into the New York stock market, because so much foreign capital had been invested, it was now questionable whether American loans could be repaid.

It seemed that only Providence or the United States Government could prevent a severe depression. But Providence, which was supposed to protect "idiots, fools and the United States," showed little concern. It was up to the business administration of Mr. Herbert Hoover. The President who had declared, "We in America today are nearer to the final triumph over poverty than ever before in the history of any land," et cetera, now saw his dovelike words of optimism return like vultures to circle over the national roost.

two "Brother, Can You Spare a Dime?"

I can observe little on the horizon today
to give us undue or great concern.
    John E. Edgerton, PRESIDENT,
    NATIONAL ASSOCIATION OF MANUFACTURERS

Some think they're strong, some think they're smart,
Like butterflies they're pulled apart,
America can break your heart.
You don't know all, sir, you don't know all.
    W. H. Auden

THAT IT happened to Herbert Hoover was a perverse trick of fate, even though he had given fate a helping hand now and then with his tariff and tax policies. For Hoover was certainly the most industrious, intelligent and forward-looking Republican to occupy the White House since Theodore Roosevelt. Born in 1874 in the little town of West Branch, Iowa, Herbert Clark Hoover had been raised a Quaker. He decided on an engineering career early in life and was graduated with honors from Stanford University in California in 1895. By the age of twenty-three he was working for a British mining company. Two years later, having worked for the company in California and in Australia, Hoover went on to China and was appointed chief engineer for the Imperial Chinese Bureau of Mines. His main function there was to

43

make certain of the efficiency and profit with which Chinese mines could be exploited by foreign companies. Success in China brought him a partnership in the British mining company and an office in London. By 1908 he had made a personal fortune and established himself as an independent consulting engineer. World War I brought him international fame—first for organizing famine relief in stricken Belgium, then as Woodrow Wilson's War Food Administrator. At the end of the war he organized famine relief throughout suffering Europe, and was as disillusioned as everyone else by the terms of the peace treaty. He became Secretary of Commerce in Harding's administration and quickly won the reputation of being the "strong man" in Washington. Continuing his job (and his role) in Coolidge's administration, he had emerged as the obvious and successful Republican candidate for President in 1928. It would seem that his entire career had been one long success story.

But Herbert Hoover was not, either by temperament or conviction, the man who could cope with a severe depression. His personality was a cold one. Josephus Daniels recalled that Hoover "seemed to regard human beings as so many numbers." William Allen White said he was "constitutionally gloomy, a congenital pessimist." Ike Hoover (a long-time White House usher) observed that the White House staff was "glad when they [the Hoovers] were gone." Secretary of State Henry L. Stimson was impressed by Hoover's austerity and lack of humor. During one and a half years of Cabinet meetings, Stimson could recall no occasion on which a joke had been cracked. Private sessions with the President were, he said, "like sitting in a bath of ink."

While the President's personality struck no sparks of human warmth, his convictions were inadequate for the task that faced him. Hoover's was a philosophy of individualism born of the loneliness of Midwestern life before the turn of the century and of his own individualistic struggle for wealth and power. But, it must be emphasized, Hoover's individualism was not the irresponsible brand represented by either Harding corruption or Coolidge indifference. Hoover saw himself as the prophet of a "New Era" (his own campaign phrase) in which businessmen,

HERBERT HOOVER

financiers, and industrialists would voluntarily undertake the responsibility of keeping the economic ship of state afloat, would
maintain employment and wages, production and credit in such
a way that the entire people would benefit. Government's role
was to aid business in every possible way to achieve these voluntary goals, not to interfere by anti-trust suits, directives, taxes, and
regulations. Technological efficiency would eventually establish
permanent prosperity. And only the nation's business leaders and
corporate technicians could bring about this efficiency. Government support for labor, farmers, the poor, or the unemployed
would only undermine that individual "get-up-and-go" instinct
which was the most valuable part of the American character. Of
course, in times of disaster, some people would need help. But
this help ought to come from voluntary local relief activities;
people's needs ought to arouse generosity in the hearts of their
more fortunate fellow citizens—for this, too, was an essential part
of the American character. And governmental activity (or labor
union activity) which threatened the freedom of businessmen to

operate "for the public good" smacked of socialism, which was to Hoover the worst of all evils. Help the top layers of society and you help (even if indirectly) the lowest layers. As for the masses of people, "The crowd only feels," Hoover wrote; "it has no mind of its own which can plan. The crowd is credulous, it destroys, it consumes, it hates, and it dreams—but it never builds."

By the spring of 1930—six months after the Crash—over 4 million Americans were out of work. And the businessmen who were to operate voluntarily for "the public good" were still responding with idiotic incantations to prosperity. "Things are better today," [November 4, 1929] said Henry Ford, "than they were yesterday." "Never before has American business been as firmly entrenched for prosperity as it is today" [December 10, 1929], said Charles M. Schwab of Bethlehem Steel. "Conditions are more favorable for permanent prosperity than they have been in the past year," added George E. Roberts of the National City Bank. When Hoover asked Andrew Mellon, Secretary of the Treasury, what he would do about the spreading depression, that multimillionaire tax evader responded, "Liquidate labor, liquidate stocks, liquidate the farmers, liquidate real estate." But Hoover did not feel he could adopt this "final solution" to the problem of the poor. Instead he called conferences. Conferences of businessmen, conferences of industrialists, conferences of financiers and bankers. Upon them he tried to urge the necessity of maintaining wages and jobs, and from them he wrung promises to maintain business as usual, as long as possible. Furthermore, Hoover asked the Federal Reserve Board to lower discount rates so as to make credit available to businessmen, and ordered the Farm Board to investigate the possibility of artificially maintaining prices for farm products. And early in 1930 Hoover backed the Smoot-Hawley Tariff Bill in Congress. This bill, which was promptly passed, raised American tariffs on foreign goods so high that it virtually ensured that foreign nations would never again be able to buy in the American market (they could not earn the dollars to do so). It also would bring about retaliatory tariffs against American exports. On March 7, 1930, Hoover proclaimed: *"All* evidences indicate that the worst effects of the crash upon unemployment will have been passed during the next sixty days." On May 1, 1930, the President said: "I am convinced we have now passed the worst." Will Rogers commented, "There has been more 'optimism' talked and less practiced than at any time during our history."

And his comment was accurate. Despite pledges to the government, the nation's business leaders saw no way to save themselves but to cut production. Some tried by cutting the work week to spread out available work among more laborers; others tried to keep their employees on by reducing wages. But the truth was that consumption had slumped tremendously. No one was buying, and more and more factories and businesses were closing their doors. During the spring of 1930 breadlines began to appear in New York, Chicago, and other American cities: long lines of patient, hopeless, humiliated men shuffling forward slowly to receive a bowl of watery soup and a crust of bread from charity kitchens, Salvation Army halls, and local relief agencies. In New York the number of families on relief was 200 per cent greater in March, 1930, than it had been in October, 1929.

Throughout the country, depression and the fear of it slowly but surely entwined icy tentacles around American society. William Green, President of the American Federation of Labor, reported that in Detroit "the men are sitting in the parks all day long and all night long, hundreds and thousands of them, muttering to themselves, out of work, seeking work." Sometimes it came abruptly—the dismissal notice in the pay envelope. Often it came slowly. First there would be a slowdown—perhaps only three days of work every week; then, sometimes, a wage cut; then, inevitably, the lay-off.

When you first started looking for a new job, your clothes neat and pressed, your shoes shined, you were fairly hopeful. You made the rounds of factories or stores. Sometimes they'd let you leave your name, but most often you'd be turned away with a gruff "No help wanted!" And soon you realized that you were not going to get a new job easily. Then, in desperation you turned to the employment agencies. You were willing to pay them a week's or a month's wages just to get a job. But the lines at the employment agencies stretched around the block, filled with worried, slightly frantic men like yourself. The employment agencies had nothing to offer either.

By now your appearance was not so neat. Your shoes were beginning to wear out through countless miles of pavement pounding. You folded up newspapers and cardboard to help the soles last. Your clothes began to look dirty (you couldn't afford to have them cleaned) and threadbare. You might wrap newspapers under your shirt to help you keep warm. But the bedraggled appearance of your clothes was nothing compared to the look of panic that now appeared in your eyes. Perhaps there were no jobs anywhere. Perhaps you'd never work again. If you were living on your savings, you wondered what would happen when the savings ran out. When they did you lived on borrowing. You borrowed from relatives and friends, and you ran credit at the local grocery store and with the landlord. But borrowing soon ended (friends and relatives were as badly off as you), and credit ran out.

Meanwhile you watched your own fear infect your family. Your wife perhaps tried to get work herself, any kind of work, as a cleaning woman or a chambermaid. But such jobs were rare, too. If any of the children were old enough to work they tried— and usually failed—to find jobs. Meat and butter and eggs were now only memories on the family table. You lived on beans and lard. You watched your children grow thin. Their clothes were now so ragged that they were ashamed to go to school. You began to pawn everything you owned, from furniture to wedding rings. You had long since lost your apartment, and you moved into ever dirtier, ever tinier quarters in ever more depressed districts. Finally, of course, you joined the breadlines and your family went on relief. They might barely survive on the three or four dollars a week that local relief agencies could afford. Or they might break up. You might go to the local poorhouse, your children to an orphanage. Or the family might scatter to stay with more fortunate relatives in the country, where food, at least, could be grown for consumption. If your children were over the age of eight or nine, they might start wandering over the countryside, looking for handouts at farmhouse doors. In the end, it would seem to you that you had never known any other life than that of a beggar. Even humiliation would be too exhausting an emotion for you; only numb hopelessness and sick despair could find room in your emaciated body. And you wondered what you'd done wrong. You wracked your brain to find out where you'd made a false turn, what sin you'd committed to earn so terrible a punishment. But if you looked around and saw the thousands and thousand of others just like yourself, you began to wonder if perhaps there wasn't something wrong with the system itself that had brought about this national catastrophe. Maybe capitalism was at fault, maybe democracy. You didn't make up your mind about that right away, but you were wondering.

In Philadelphia, in 1930, children starved. In Chicago, bands of homeless men slept on the lower level of Wacker Drive, huddled together around camp fires built of straw and scraps, against the cold. In New York, thousands of men, some with families, some without, began building little huts for themselves out of cardboard cartons or scraps of tin and wood along the Hudson River, below Riverside Drive. Gangs of desperate men were seen in towns and cities across the nation, fighting over choice morsels at municipal garbage dumps.

During the autumn of 1930, the Northwest apple growers had an inspiration. Since they had a large crop of apples, and no one to buy them, they organized their distribution among the jobless for resale on street corners. Thus appeared the shivering, ragged apple sellers in American cities. Standing over pitiful wooden crates of apples, they silently beseeched the more fortunate passerby to buy an apple—for a nickel, but perhaps for more, if the buyer was charitable. The Bureau of the Census classified these half-begging apple sellers as "employed." President Hoover later insisted: "Many persons left their jobs for the more profitable one of selling apples." So desperate were conditions in New York City that from faraway Africa, the natives of the Cameroons collected $3.77 which they sent to the city authorities for "the relief of the starving." By midwinter (a harsh and severe winter) of 1931, over eight million Americans were unemployed. By December, 1931, unemployment reached 13.5 million—almost one third of the American labor force. What were these people to do?

Many of them hit the road. Accompanied by families, in broken-down old cars or, increasingly, alone, jobless workers roamed from town to town, city to city, state to state, seeking work that was unavailable. The transient knew in his bones that things were no better ahead than they had been behind, but somehow the movement itself seemed positive. It was something, however hopeless a thing, to *do*.

These migrants were not traditional hobos. The old-time hobo, following the sun, did as little work as possible. His object was to reduce his needs so that he would not have to work. But Depression migrants were desperately seeking work. No one ever knew how many transients appeared during the Depression, but estimates run to one million. The Southern Pacific Railroad, for example, reported that it had ejected nearly 700,000 vagrants from its trains (boxcars) in 1932.

It was a rough life. When you tired of walking you waited in the ditch near a railroad embankment (preferably near a station so that passing trains would be going slowly). Then the dash to an open-doored boxcar as it passed. If you missed you might be crippled or killed beneath the steel wheels. Inside you were sure to find at least a few fellow bums sitting in the darkness waiting to jump off, into nowhere in particular. And you had to keep an eye out for the railroad "bulls," the private police hired by railroad companies to keep transients out of their boxcars. If the bulls caught you they'd beat you with their sticks, perhaps kill you, or turn you over to a local sheriff. If this happened down South, in Georgia or Florida, for example, you were sent to the chain gang. But if you avoided the bulls and jumped from the boxcar before the train stopped and made a dash for it, you'd be welcome in the nearest hobo "jungle." These jungles, which were to be found everywhere in the United States, were hobo camps where the derelicts had constructed cardboard or driftwood shacks. There was no sanitation, no garbage collection (and very, very little garbage), no water except what could be hauled from a nearby creek. And wherever you went, there was no work. Once in a while you found yourself chopping wood or doing other chores for some kindly farmer, or you might, in some states (especially California), get a job in state labor camps run by local authorities and equipped by the U. S. Army. But mostly, if you found work it was under tremendously exploitive conditions—picking fruit on some huge commercial farm for five cents an hour (which you might or might not receive at the end of the day, depending on the whim of the overseer), or working in mills and factories as a scab (a man who worked at a strike-bound plant) for four dollars a week. To eat, when you had no work, you rummaged in garbage dumps, or you stole.

In some respects it was the children who suffered most. Millions of them dropped out of school, hundreds of thousands lost their families. And while parents starved themselves to see that their children got what little food was available, often this was not enough. A Chicago social worker, distressed by a report from Chicago's Children's Memorial Hospital that a child had just died there of starvation, reported in 1932 that children in that city were "cold and hungry and lacking security and developing physical conditions sure to bring on tuberculosis, and other maladies, and mental attitudes sure to bring on delinquency." Child labor, under appalling sweat-shop conditions, reappeared even in the few areas where it was illegal.

And as despair settled like a dark pall over workers in and from the cities, so, too, during 1930 and 1931, it deepened among the nation's farmers. The Wall Street Crash had worsened the plight of farmers who had already been through a decade of diminishing income. Farm prices fell 30 per cent during the first two years of the Depression. Corn sold for 15 cents a bushel, cotton and wool went for 5 cents a pound, hogs brought 3 cents, and beef 2.5 cents a pound. And farmers didn't know what to do about it—except keep production up, or actually increase it, thereby adding to the slide in prices. Industry could always cut back production to maintain prices, but in 1929 and 1930 farmers feared to cut back production: it required every scrap of produce they could raise just to keep them going at those prices. Farm income, nationwide, fell by 33 per cent from 1929 to 1931.

But the farmer's debts did not fall. Both his taxes and his mortgages had been figured and assumed during the twenties, when farm prices were higher. A farmer who had borrowed, for example, $1,000 on a mortgage when his cotton sold for 15 cents a pound owed, in effect, 6,666 pounds of cotton, but when suddenly the bottom fell out and cotton was worth 5 cents a pound he owed almost 20,000 pounds of cotton. Furthermore, many of the banks which ultimately owned farm mortgages had taken heavy losses either through loans or speculation on the stock market. They could afford less and less to postpone foreclosures.

The countryside showed it. Fences sagging in disrepair, fields unplowed, worn-out farm machinery, unpainted buildings, starving animals. Some farmers found it cheaper to burn crops than to pay to have them hauled to market. William Allen White wrote, "Every farmer, whether his farm is under mortgage or not, knows that with farm products priced as they are today, sooner or later he must go down."

When he did go down—when the sheriff arrived with the dispossess notice, when the auctioneer arrived to sell off the homestead that had taken generations to build—the farmer joined the flow of aimless vagrants heading down roads leading nowhere. He didn't know what had hit him. Something had gone wrong among the money men back East, and he'd never trusted them anyhow. But this time it looked as if they meant to finish him off. The American farmer during 1930 and 1931 must have been grimly amused to see Red Cross food centers sprouting across some of the richest agricultural land in the world to pass out food to starving farmers and their families.

As the second winter of depression deepened, the local relief organizations in cities and towns began to run out of money. Most cities had no regular relief organization. Private charities and public poorhouses had generally been competent to care for those who were out of work. During normal times the unemployed were, by and large, the unemployable. And they were treated as charity cases. But private charity could not cope with the flood of starving people which engulfed the nation during 1931. Many towns and cities had organized public relief programs in 1930, but local taxes and other financial resources were not enough to provide more than a bare subsistence for the masses who were now in need. It seemed that only the federal government could provide the necessary help if thousands of people were not to starve.

But President Hoover remained firmly wedded to his conviction that federal aid was federal interference, that federal relief funds for the states would somehow undermine local initiative. Therefore Hoover inaugurated an advertising campaign carried out by his Organization on Unemployment Relief, to promote private and local charity. The new organization was headed by Walter S. Gifford, President of the American Telephone and Telegraph Company. So slight were the Organization's efforts on behalf of the unemployed that when, in January, 1932, Gifford was questioned by a Senate investigating committee, he had to admit that he did not even know how many people were unemployed, or what the resources were with which local agencies could meet the problem. Nobody had informed Mr. Gifford that New York City, the richest in the country, could now afford to give only $2.39 per week for relief to an entire family. He seemed unaware that huge areas of the country had no relief agencies whatsoever. But he remained convinced of one thing: federal aid would be a positive disservice to the needy.

American businessmen generally agreed with Gifford, although some were beginning to have doubts. Most continued to issue ridiculous statements about imminent prosperity. Most thought that this depression, like so many before it, would soon blow over. Most echoed the sentiments expressed by the United States Chamber of Commerce, which attempted to reassure the country by pointing out that after all, "we have had at least seventeen of these cycles of depression in the last 120 years." Charles Mitchell of the National City Bank remarked, "So long as we live under a system of individual liberty, we are bound to have fluctuations in business." And Albert Wiggin of the Chase National Bank, when asked by Senator Robert La Follette whether there was no way to prevent depressions, replied: "There is no commission or any brain in the world that can prevent it." Shocked, La Follette demanded to know if Wiggin thought the capacity for human suffering was unlimited. "I think so," the banker answered.

Businessmen also opposed relief for the needy. To them it smacked of England's infamous "dole." If government, whether local, state, or federal, undertook to keep people from starving, then those people would grow lazy and, presumably flourishing on their bowl of cabbage soup every day, refuse to work for wages. But this was only in theory. In practice, businessmen were not heartless ogres. They were usually the heaviest contributors to community relief projects. And many attempted to come up with schemes by which private enterprise could help the unemployed.

For example, John B. Nichols, President of the Oklahoma Gas Utilities Company, suggested in a letter to his friend Patrick J. Hurley, Hoover's Secretary of War, that restaurants be asked to dump food left on plates into five-gallon containers. The local unemployed could then earn these five-gallon containers of garbage by chopping wood for local farmers. Hurley was very much impressed by this scheme and urged it upon the government. But not even Hoover would go that far.

Businessmen were confused, to say the least. Nothing in either their personal or corporate past experience had equipped them to understand what was happening to the nation, much less to suggest remedies for it. Feeling uneasily that they ought to appear optimistic, they kept uttering clichés. Charles M. Schwab of Bethlehem Steel advised, "Just grin, keep on working." Walter Gifford offered this thought: "What we must have is faith, hope and charity." Myron C. Taylor of United States Steel thought: "We shall have learned something of high importance [out of the Depression]. It is too soon to say just what we are learning."

Sewell Avery of Montgomery Ward and Company admitted sadly: "To describe the causes of this situation is rather beyond my capacity. I am unfortunate in having no friends that seem to be able to explain it clearly to me." On the other hand, Daniel Willard, of the Baltimore and Ohio Railroad, was clear about one thing; "I would steal before I would starve," he announced.

Some businessmen and their friends, however, were beginning to wonder about the system which had made them wealthy. President Nicholas Murray Butler of Columbia University, an arch conservative, warned in 1931 that planning in industry was now essential. "Gentlemen," he pointed out, "if we wait too long, somebody will come forward with a solution that we may not like." Paul Mazur of Lehman Brothers agreed. "The tragic lack of planning that characterizes the capitalistic system," he wrote, "is a reflection upon the intelligence of everyone . . ."

The nation's intellectuals agreed with that conclusion. Long disowned by a society they had detested when it was wealthy, American intellectuals saw the crash and the onslaught of depression as a judgment on years of greed and a proof that the American system was basically rotten. It seemed that H. L. Mencken had been right about democracy, that it "consists almost wholly of the discovery, chase and scotching of bugaboos. The statesman becomes, in the last analysis, a mere witch-hunter, a glorified smeller and snooper, eternally chanting 'Fe, Fi, Fo, Fum.' " As for Congressmen, Mencken dismissed the typical people's representative as "A knavish and preposterous nonentity, half way between a kleagle of the Ku Klux Klan and a grand worthy of the Knights of Zoroaster. It is such vermin who make the laws of the United States." And democracy itself was meaningless; "All the known facts lie flatly against it," Mencken proclaimed. Mencken was not speaking for himself alone; he expertly voiced the unspoken opinions of many intellectuals. And their opinions were an advance barometric warning of public opinion in general.

As time went on and depression worsened and the federal government continued to sit on its hands, people were growing angry, dangerously angry. Incidents were multiplying across the nation. On March 19, 1930, 1,100 men standing in a breadline in New York seized two truckloads of bread and rolls as they were being delivered to a nearby hotel. In Henryetta, Oklahoma, in July, 1931, three hundred jobless men threatened to beat up and kill local storekeepers unless they were given food; they got their food. In Detroit, in 1932, it was a common occurrence for unemployed men to smash shop windows at night and loot stores. In that same city, two families who resisted eviction by shooting and killing a landlord were later acquitted of murder by sympathetic jurors.

Revolution was not imminent, except in the imaginations of a few hopeful radicals, in 1931. But as humorist Will Rogers warned, "You let this country go hungry, and they are going to eat no matter what happens to Budgets, Income Taxes or Wall Street values. Washington mustn't forget who rules when it comes to a showdown." Lillian Wald, founder and director of New York City's famed Henry Street Settlement House, demanded: "Have you ever heard a hungry child cry? Have you seen the uncontrollable trembling of parents who have gone half starved for weeks so that the children may have food?" But Herbert Hoover had not, in fact, heard or seen such things in America. "Nobody," he told newspaper reporters, "is actually starving. The hobos, for example, are better fed than they have ever been. One hobo in New York got ten meals in one day." Remarks like that have been, historically, in other countries, the building blocks of revolution. Could it happen in America? Will Rogers was a perceptive observer; it could. As 1931 drew to its disastrous end, the atmosphere of America was thick with despair and anger, heavy with muttered threats.

three Year of Crisis

What the country needs is a good, big laugh. There
seems to be a condition of hysteria. If someone
could get off a good joke every ten days, I think
our troubles would be over.

Herbert Hoover

You tried to teach men love. Lip-service many give.
Look down, oh Lord, and see Yourself the lives we live.

Bonus Expeditionary Force Newspaper

THE YEAR 1932 opened with a sense of crisis in the air. Now the
unemployment figure had reached 14 million, and was still rising
rapidly. National income had declined by 50 per cent (from
$87.5 to $41.7 billion) since those remote and faintly incredible
days of 1929. Manufacturing had declined by more than 50 per
cent; the American economy was grinding to a standstill. And
those who still retained jobs were earning, for example, 5 cents
an hour in saw mills and $2.39 for a fifty-hour work week in tex-
tile mills; children in Connecticut were earning 75 cents a week
for fifty-five hours of hard work in certain sweatshops. Now the
breadlines included former shopkeepers, former businessmen,
former middle-class housewives. But local relief agencies could
no longer support the burden; by 1932 only one quarter of America's unemployed were actually receiving help.

In New York City unemployed men, overflowing their shanty
towns along Riverside Drive, had now moved into Central Park.

There they built shacks and scavenged for scraps among the city's garbage dumps. In Chicago, one out of every two workers was unemployed, and Mayor Anton Cermak, begging for federal aid, warned Washington that it might be better to send $150 million now than federal troops later on. Philadelphia life was described as one of "slow starvation and progressive disintegration of family life." In the Pennsylvania coal fields miners lived on roots and dandelions. In Kentucky people ate weeds. In California children were dying of starvation.

And as public money for relief ran out, many rich Americans opposed increased taxes to help the needy or, more commonly, evaded those taxes they were supposed to pay. Thus, Colonel Robert R. McCormick, owner of the *Chicago Tribune* (and of much else in Illinois), reported his personal property holdings for tax purposes as amounting to no more than $25,250. Silas Strawn of the United States Chamber of Commerce reported property holdings which called for only $120 in taxes; Louis Florsheim of the Florsheim Shoe Company had only $90 worth of taxable property, evidently. J. P. Morgan paid no income tax at all in 1932. Samuel Insull, the great Chicago financier, suddenly resigned his eighty-five directorships and sixty-five chairmanships of corporations and took a trip to Europe. In September of 1932, a Cook County grand jury indicted him for embezzlement. The leaders of American business and finance were quite obviously not about to take responsibility for the national welfare.

On March 7, 1932, in freezing weather, three thousand jobless men marched on the shut-down Ford plants at River Rouge in Dearborn. They were an orderly, even a dispirited crowd at first, simply demanding work. But when they reached the plants, Dearborn police ordered them to turn back. The men wanted to present a petition at the plant. When they pressed on the police opened up on them with tear-gas bombs. Members of the crowd began to throw rocks and pieces of ice. The Ford Company fire department now unleashed tons of high-pressure icy cold water on the marchers from fire hoses. Then the police opened fire with pistols, rifles, and machine guns. The crowd fled in panic (although some tried to drag away their wounded), leaving four dead behind. A few days later, many thousands of Detroit workers marched behind four coffins beneath red banners and signs which read "FORD GAVE BULLETS FOR BREAD." The disruption of American society into open class warfare might well be signaled by a few more such riots. In Mississippi, a local politician named Theodore G. Bilbo remarked, "Folks are restless. Communism is gaining a foothold. Right here in Mississippi some people are about ready to lead a mob. In fact, I'm getting a little pink myself."

Herbert Hoover's chief weapon during 1932 to combat depression was the Reconstruction Finance Corporation. Established on the theory that the government ought to lend money to industries and businesses in order to keep them going, the RFC was authorized to make loans to banks (which would then, presumably, be better able to lend money to businessmen). RFC loans were kept secret at first, ostensibly because to announce them might cause the public to lose confidence in the banks receiving loans. But in 1932, Congress forced the RFC to disclose its operations. What Congress learned was hardly reassuring. For instance, in June, 1932, RFC President Charles G. Dawes had resigned to re-enter private business. He took over direction of the Central Republic Bank in Chicago, and a few weeks later the RFC suddenly loaned the Central Republic Bank $90 million. Furthermore, the man who succeeded Dawes as President of RFC authorized a loan of $12 million to a Cleveland bank of which he was a director. By the end of 1932, the RFC had become thoroughly discredited.

In 1930, the Democrats had won control of both the Senate and the House of Representatives. During the last two years of Hoover's administration many progressive Senators and Representatives tried to force new measures on the reluctant President. But Hoover fought a desperate rear-guard action for his philosophy of local self-help and federal non-interference. Reform and relief legislation continued to appear to him as a threat to the

"American way of life." As he had said in 1931, Hoover believed that "The sole function of government is to bring about a condition of affairs favorable to the beneficial development of private enterprise."

So when Senator George W. Norris of Nebraska and Representative Fiorello LaGuardia of New York pushed a law through Congress which made "yellow dog" contracts in industry partly, if not wholly, illegal, Hoover fought the measure desperately and signed it only under protest. When Hoover's own Farm Board warned farmers that they had to reduce planting if they hoped to maintain farm prices, the President undermined all efforts of the Board to exercise crop control. When Senator Robert F. Wagner of New York and Representative John Nance Garner of Texas passed a bill through Congress which authorized the RFC to lend $300 million to local and state relief agencies, Hoover first vetoed the bill and then reluctantly signed it when it was repassed in different form. But, the President said, "These loans are to be based upon absolute need . . . I do not expect any state to resort to it [RFC] except as a last extremity." By the end of 1932, RFC had allocated only $30 million of its $300 million for relief.

By now public hatred and contempt for Herbert Hoover had reached proportions possibly unique in the history of the Republic's opinions of its Presidents. The shanty towns and tarpaper shack villages huddled along railroad embankments throughout the country were called "Hoovervilles." Broken-down automobiles hauled by mules were called "Hoover wagons," empty pockets were "Hoover flags," newspapers became "Hoover blankets." The cold personality of the man in the White House became a symbol of all that was most hateful in American life. Yet Herbert Hoover could not help his personality. "I can't be a Theodore Roosevelt," Hoover admitted sadly, "and I have no Wilsonian qualities."

Hoover's sole passion, it seemed, was to keep the national budget balanced. If the government spent more money than it received and showed a deficit in its budget, then businessmen and financiers would, supposedly, lose confidence in it. If they did that, they would refuse to invest in the national economy (after all, if the deficit became large enough, perhaps one day the federal government would be unable to pay back the money it had borrowed through the sale of government bonds and securities, would be unable to pay its employees, would go bankrupt, thereby making its currency worthless), and that would only make the Depression more severe. But although he favored government economy, Hoover did not favor being penny wise and pound foolish where it really mattered. In the spring of 1932, he sent a secret message to Congress advising it not to cut the pay of Army and Navy personnel because the government might soon need its troops to put down revolution.

It wasn't a revolution that came, although to many semi-literate conservatives and frightened businessmen it looked like the beginning of "the Red terror." What came instead was the BEF —the Bonus Expeditionary Force. It all started in Portland, Oregon. In May, 1932, some World War I veterans in Portland decided that since they were living on the edge of starvation, now was as good a time as any for Congress to pay them the bonuses they had been promised for their service in the war "to make the world safe for democracy." Congress had originally voted, just after the war, to pay these bonuses in the year 1945. But by 1945, or 1933 for that matter, many veterans felt they would have succumbed to hunger. They needed the money then, not twenty-two years hence, and Congress had decided that the country owed them that anyhow. Choosing as their leader an unemployed former sergeant named Walter W. Waters, the Portland veterans decided to publicize their cause by marching on Washington and petitioning Congress or the President directly for prompt payment of the bonus. Maintaining strict discipline (the Bonus marchers allowed "no panhandling, no drinking, no radicalism") the men set out—walking sometimes, riding freight cars sometimes, eating what they could get from friendly folks along the way or going hungry.

An incident in East St. Louis made the Portland Bonus March

front-page news. There, railroad bulls prevented the men from boarding a Baltimore and Ohio freight train heading east. When the veterans refused to leave the freight yards, units of the Illinois National Guard were summoned to drive them out. Many veterans, now hearing for the first time of the Bonus March, decided to join in. From New York and Chicago, from San Francisco and Los Angeles, from Denver, Miami, Detroit, New Orleans, from every state and a thousand towns and villages they began the long trek to Washington, D.C. Lean men mostly, some bringing their wives and children (they had no place to leave them), recapturing that dusty spring some of the comradeship they'd known years before in France, singing the old war songs, "Mademoiselle from Armentières," or "Tipperary," they trudged down all the nation's highways towards that big white dome in the capital.

By the time Waters and the Portland men reached Washington, their number had grown to 1,000. In the days and weeks that followed, new contingents arrived until about 15,000 veterans and some families had joined them. They established a rough camp on the marshy land across the Anacostia River known as Anacostia Flats. There they built shanties of scrap wood and tin, or cardboard, dug latrines (everything was done with a pathetic attention to old army regulations), and made out as best they could.

The superintendent of Washington's Metropolitan Police Force was a retired Army officer himself. Pelham D. Glassford had been the youngest American Brigadier General in France in 1918. He liked the veterans, understood something of their comradeship, sympathized with their needs. He got them fed by requisitioning Army field kitchens, made sure that his police treated them respectfully, and, as he rode around Anacostia Flats on his big blue Harley-Davidson motorcycle, he kidded the veterans, talked with them, did what he could to maintain their morale.

And their morale needed maintaining. The House of Representatives had been debating a bill to pay the veterans their bonus immediately. On June 15, 1932, with the BEF camped not far away, the House passed the bill. But the Senate took a stricter view of things. Senators were quite used to the normal kind of lobbyist—the agent of some industry or business who passed out cigars and drinks and other "favors" in return for the protection of his client's interests in "the greatest deliberative assembly on earth." But they were not used to lobbyists who wore tattered old Army uniforms and had no favors to pass out. The Bonus Army, the Senate felt, was a threat. To pass the Bonus Bill would be to knuckle under to mob violence. Besides, it would unbalance the budget. When, on June 17, the Bonus Bill came up for a vote in the Senate, apprehensive members of the Hoover administration wondered if it wasn't time to call out the Army. Thousands of veterans had gathered outside the Capitol building. But Police Superintendent Glassford talked the nervous administrators out of any display of force. Finally, after hours of waiting, the news was brought out. "Comrades," Waters cried out, "I have bad news." The Bonus Bill had been defeated. As the crowd of men began to grumble, he shouted, "Comrades, let us show them that we are patriotic Americans. I call on you to sing 'America.' " The men sang. Then they quietly dispersed to return to their shanties in Anacostia Flats.

Hardly a reign of Red terror. But what to do next? Some of the veterans and their families began to drift away from the encampment, back onto the dusty roads leading nowhere. But very many stayed on. Perhaps their continued presence in Washington might somehow get the government to change its mind. And anyhow, Anacostia Flats, for all its poor sanitation, scanty food, and "Hooverville" shacks, was the only home they had.

Some Congressmen had said that the BEF was under Communist domination. But this was patently a lie. There were scattered Communist agitators among them, and Communist leaflets were occasionally distributed. But the mood of the veterans was distinctly anti-Communist. Communist leaflets were burned whenever they were found, and Communist agitators were beaten up and thrown out of the encampment. Although there was no doubt that the Communist Party viewed the BEF as an important chance to recruit members, its influence was nil. When John T. Pace, the Communist leader, tried to speak to the veterans he was nearly mobbed by them. Only the intervention of Police Superintendent Glassford ("Pace has just as much right to speak here as anyone") saved him from violence.

As July dragged by in terrible heat, with the men feeling useless and the women and children trying to make the best of encampment life, the BEF depended more and more on Glassford. When food supplies ran short he bought more with $1,000 of his own money. To reporters he said, "Why, some of those boys soldiered for me; they're my boys." When whites and Negroes squabbled and fought, Glassford broke them apart personally, saying on one occasion, "We're all veterans together and there'll be no fighting among veterans!" In July, Anacostia Flats celebrated the birth of its first baby, Bernard Myers. But increasingly the veterans felt their battle was lost. Congress would adjourn soon and that would be the end of it. Furthermore, President Hoover had steadfastly refused to receive any veterans' representatives at the White House, or to visit them, or to even acknowledge their existence. On the last day of Congress, with the veterans once more crowding Capitol Hill, Hoover canceled his scheduled visit to the Senate to avoid seeing the assembled veterans even from a distance.

Glassford had hoped to evacuate the men and families at Anacostia Flats to camps in the nearby countryside. There, he hoped, the veterans might be able to do subsistence farming and even set up light, cooperative manufacturing. Every day many veterans were drifting away from Anacostia; Glassford's idea might provide those who remained with new hope.

But the District of Columbia Commissioners, Secretary of War Patrick J. Hurley, most of the administration, and President Hoover himself, felt that the encampment at Anacostia Flats was a revolutionary threat to the American government. Besides, it looked bad to visiting foreign dignitaries, was messy, and was

the face of a nation

Real estate developments flourished outside every American city during the thirties. Known as "Hoovervilles," they displayed Yankee ingenuity at its best. If there were few conveniences, at least there was no rent.

And they were usually close to marketing areas, known in those days as "free food dumps." The choice of food was somewhat limited and the ration was small, but there were no check-out counters.

Some people kept up with the rent, somehow—

Others took to the road to enjoy outdoor life.

There was time to think things over. This man said: "No man in the United States has had the trouble I had since 1931. No man. Don't talk to me. I'm deaf. I lost my farm in 1931. I went into town to work with a painter. I fell off a scaffold and broke my leg. I went to work in an acid factory. I got acid spilt on me; burnt my nose and made me blind. Then I get those awful headaches. I've been to lots of doctors, but that doesn't help me. They come on at sundown. No man in the United States has had the trouble I had since 1931."

Not that there wasn't *some* work to be had. Children below the age of 10 could often earn as much as 25¢ a day working ten hours in the cranberry bogs of New Jersey.

And Americans still sought to improve themselves through education,

even in "separate but equal" schools down South.

When the dust storms blew away the soil, the tremendous dignity of earlier generations of pioneers still showed in American faces.

Like their forefathers before them, they loaded up their belongings and headed west—to where they were told the sun set over a better land.

But the road was a long one—

And the American dream mocked them every step of the way.

a potential breeding ground for disease. On July 28, there was a confused but minor riot when policemen, under District Commission orders, cleared some veterans out of unused old buildings on Pennsylvania Avenue. Jittery police killed two veterans, but a riot was averted by Glassford's hurried arrival and calming words. Nonetheless, the administration decided that a state of insurrection existed. Hurley called upon Army Chief of Staff Douglas MacArthur to use troops to clear out the veterans. MacArthur picked up his riding crop, summoned his aide, a Major Dwight D. Eisenhower, mounted his white horse, and set about his business.

Late in the afternoon, the veterans at Anacostia Flats saw four troops of cavalry with drawn sabers, six tanks, and a long column of infantry with fixed bayonets, gas masks and tear-gas bombs on their belts, bearing down on them. The troops paused for exactly one hour to permit the veterans to snatch up their pathetic belongings and start running. Then, as evening fell, they moved in, prodding men with their bayonets, tossing tear-gas bombs ahead of them, and setting fire to the broken-down shacks and shanties along the way.

Women and children scrambled frantically from the path of the soldiers, coughing and crying from the tear gas. Seven-year-old Eugene King tried to snatch his pet rabbit from his tent, but was bayoneted in the leg by a soldier ("Get out of here, you son-of-a-bitch"); Joe Angelo, a veteran from Camden, New Jersey, watched as cavalry officer George S. Patton led his men in destroying Angelo's shack. Angelo had saved Patton's life on the Western Front years before. As their ramshackle homes went up in flames, the veterans and their wives and children streamed into Maryland and safety. Behind them they left the wounded, their illusions, and little Bernard Myers, the bonus baby, who died in a Washington hospital from tear-gas inhalation.

To Douglas MacArthur it was a famous victory. "I have released in my day," the General said, "more than one community which had been held in the grip of a foreign enemy." The Hoover administration issued statements that the BEF had been a horde of criminals and Communists. But later investigations, even those carried out by the administration itself, failed to substantiate any such charges. Police Commissioner Glassford was dismissed, and when a group of writers, headed by Sherwood Anderson, went to the White House to protest the use of soldiers against unarmed veterans Hoover refused to see them. MacArthur was right, in a sense. The victory was to become famous. Its fame was to haunt those who had won it all the rest of their lives.

That summer of 1932, farmers in Iowa blockaded roads, armed themselves with pitchforks and shotguns, and refused to allow farm produce to go to market. Dairy farmers dumped milk into Midwestern roads rather than see it sold for 2 cents a quart and then resold by distributors for 8 cents a quart. Throughout the nation, despair had turned to deep resentment and dismay into anger. Revolution was not yet anywhere in sight. But voices of fear were being heard increasingly across the land. Congressman Hamilton Fish, Jr., of New York warned his colleagues: "I am trying to provide security for human beings which they are not getting. If we don't give it under the existing system, the people will change the system. Make no mistake about that." Senator David A. Reed of Pennsylvania observed: ". . . if this country ever needed a Mussolini, it needs one now." Publisher Bernarr Macfadden called for martial law.

But as the sense of crisis deepened, there remained one hope. 1932 was a Presidential election year. Perhaps the old machinery of American politics could be used, as it had been at times of crisis in the past, to solve the people's problems. Perhaps the political parties would offer new programs, new leaders who could find peaceful solutions, democratic solutions to the problems posed by depression. Many felt that 1932 was American democracy's last chance to justify itself. If it failed, the people would surely change the system—perhaps to the left, perhaps to the right—but if the existence of personal liberty could not be reconciled with the need for economic security, there was little doubt that personal liberty would suffer. And if democracy lost in America, what chance would it have in the rest of the world?

Mussolini had already established his Facist government in Italy; in Germany the formerly comical little man with the Charlie Chaplin mustache, Adolf Hitler, was now moving boldly to seize the reins of power. In Russia the people had long since sacrificed liberty for security. Would they do the same, eventually, in the United States?

Already many of the country's richest men had converted their dollars to gold or jewels or Swiss francs and were busily shipping their wealth away to safer vaults. It was rumored that luxury yachts at Miami and other East Coast ports had their steam up continuously, ready to carry their owners to safety at a moment's notice. And potential leaders were beginning to appear on the scene. In Detroit, an aggressive and very articulate priest named Father Coughlin was building up a tremendous radio audience for his program of "social justice." Down in Louisiana, Governor Huey Long had already made himself a virtual dictator, relying on the appeal of his "every-man-a-king" program. A tough rabble-rouser named Gerald L. K. Smith was about to join Long's following and add his own ideas to Long's. The Communist Party had doubled its membership from 6,000 in 1929 to 12,000 in 1932, and although it had so far failed dismally to take real advantage of such opportunities as the Bonus March, it was always possible that it might find intelligent leadership one day. In the Midwest, scattered groups of young men were organizing themselves into "khaki-shirt" semi-military outfits. All these voices were not by any means representative of the overwhelming body of American public opinion. But they were symptoms of a dread disease. And if their clamor never rose to the level of a political shout, it was because there were other voices to be heard in America in 1932: the voices of an older tradition of American reform. Liberalism and Progressivism, so long muffled by a decade of reaction and irresponsibility, were speaking with increasing urgency to a larger and larger audience.

four The Emergence
of the New Deal

"Promised, promised, promised, promised, promised,"
say the leaves across America . . . And everywhere,
through the immortal dark, something moving in the
night, and something stirring in the hearts of men . . .
Thomas Wolfe

I pledge you, I pledge myself,
to a new deal for the American People.
Franklin D. Roosevelt

THROUGH THE tarnished brilliance of the twenties and the deepening gloom of Depression years the statements of most men of power and leadership in the United States might have given an observer the impression that serious political and economic thought was dead. It was not; it simply had no base of political power from which to act. But not a few men of vision had cherished ideals of reform and progress through the long night of complacency and reaction. Their ideas and dreams arose from several different sources.

First, there were the inheritors of Theodore Roosevelt's Progressivism. Despite the fact that he was a Republican President, Teddy Roosevelt, during the years after his terms of office, had come to believe that the Republican Party, in the grip of businessmen and industrialists, could not be a weapon of reform.

Expressing himself on the subject of the men who controlled Republican policy, he said: "I certainly have no especial respect or admiration for, and no trust in, the typical big moneyed men of my country . . . with ideals which in their essence are merely those of so many glorified pawn brokers." During his Presidency Roosevelt had earned a reputation (somewhat less than justified) as a "trust-buster" because he had in several instances brought suit against giant industrial combines under the provisions of the Sherman Anti-Trust Law. But later, Roosevelt came to believe that it was not so much bigness in industry itself which threatened the national welfare, as the *unregulated* power of big business. When he finally bolted the Republican Party and ran for President on the Independent Progressive "Bull Moose" ticket in 1912, the party program called for conservation of natural resources, public ownership of public utilities, and government regulation of large industries. Roosevelt was defeated in 1912, but many of his followers, such as Senator George W. Norris of Nebraska, Henry L. Stimson (Secretary of War, 1911–1913), Gifford Pinchot (Roosevelt's Chief of Forestry in the Department of Agriculture), William Allen White (world-famed editor of the Emporia, Kansas, *Gazette*), Norman Thomas (later leader of the Socialist Party), Felix Frankfurter (the liberal lawyer and professor of law), and others, clung to the Progressive visions of their youth.

During the election campaigns of 1912 and 1916, Woodrow Wilson and the Democratic Party had appropriated many of Roosevelt's ideas and some of his followers. Almost all of the Progressive program was included in Woodrow Wilson's "New Freedom." But while Progressives thought in terms of regulating big business enterprises, Wilson and his followers did not believe that large industrial empires could ever be successfully controlled. Instead they had to be broken up or, in certain cases, owned outright by the public. Competition between businesses was the only way to guarantee economic liberty, and where competition was strangled by the huge size of corporations, government had to step in to break up monopoly. It was within the framework of the New Freedom, too, that the older followers of William Jennings Bryan (who was Secretary of State in Wilson's Cabinet from 1913 to 1915) found refuge from the political storms. The Bryan men were the inheritors of the old American agrarian reform movements and Bryan's own unsuccessful Populist movement with its insistence on cheap money for the farmers and a lower tariff. But Bryan and certain of the Progressives split with Wilson over America's entry into World War I. They feared that war would undermine efforts at reform, and their fears were later justified. Nonetheless, under the Wilsonian banners to the bitter end remained such men as Louis Brandeis, William G. McAdoo (Secretary of the Treasury, 1913–1918), Cordell Hull (Representative in Congress from Tennessee), John Nance Garner and Sam Rayburn (Representatives from Texas), Homer Cummings (Connecticut District Attorney), and Franklin Delano Roosevelt (Assistant Secretary of the Navy, 1913–1920). Six months before his death in 1924, Woodrow Wilson said, "The world has been made safe for democracy, but democracy has not yet made the world safe against irrational revolution. That supreme task, which is nothing less than the salvation of civilization, now faces democracy, insistent, imperative." The way to avoid revolution, Wilson felt, was through social justice. "This," he said, "is what our age is blindly feeling in its reaction against what it deems the too great selfishness of the capitalistic system." Cast out into the political wilderness by the Republican victories of the twenties, the Wilsonians continued to develop their ideas, adapting them to new conditions.

Yet another source of reform ideas came from the developing science of sociology and the long, long work of social welfare. Social welfare work, sometimes known as the "social gospel," had started in the late nineteenth century as a non-political attempt to alleviate, through private or local public efforts, the miseries and injustices inflicted upon the poorest people by the newly powerful industrial system. Enlisting Christianity on the side of reform, Walter Rauschenbusch, a Protestant theologian, preached: "If the banner of the Kingdom of God is to enter through the gates of the future, it will have to be carried by the tramping hosts of labor." And many dedicated men and women heeded these words. Jane Addams established Hull House in Chicago as a refuge for the poor, Lillian Wald set up the Henry Street Settlement in New York City, and their work was copied in cities throughout the country. Social welfare workers gave America its first real picture of and thorough contact with working-class life; they exposed child labor, starvation wages, industrial accidents, yellow-dog contracts—the entire machinery of exploitation by which thousands of dollars were made for the few and thousands of workers destroyed in the process. Such women social workers as Frances Perkins, Mary Dewson, and Edith Abbott were derisively termed "dedicated old maids." But it was through their work that the struggles for minimum-wage laws, laws against child labor, and laws against sweatshops first got started. And it was from social welfare sources that such men as Henry Morgenthau, Jr., Herbert Lehman, Adolf A. Berle, Jr., Charles A. Beard, John Dewey, Sidney Hillman, Harry Hopkins, Alfred E. Smith, Robert F. Wagner, and Franklin D. Roosevelt first received their practical education in the human cost of capitalism.

Finally, reform and Progressivism during the twenties found a natural refuge in the American universities and emerged with new ideas in 1932. Economists such as William T. Foster and Waddill Catchings pointed out that the whole classical economic theory of the operation of free industry was a delusion. According to classical theory, the money invested in industrial enterprise, by being paid out eventually to workers (both in the enterprise and in its many suppliers), automatically provided the workers with the money with which to purchase the products of industry —a sort of perpetual motion machine, provided production was maintained. But, according to Foster and Catchings, industry did not, in fact, seriously increase wages as efficiency increased. Furthermore, both individuals and corporations had to save money, too, thereby removing it from circulation. Thus production would outstrip consumption, and depression would result. The economists pointed out, for example, that Henry Ford had never, in

REXFORD GUY TUGWELL

any single year, paid out enough in wages to enable his workers to buy the cars that rolled off the Ford assembly lines. Prosperity depended on a large volume of money being made available for consumer spending. If necessary the government itself would have to make that money available. For economic thinker Thorstein Veblen, whose works were tremendously influential among liberals and reformers, business was the enemy. Veblen made a distinction between industry (the production of goods) and business (the sale or distribution of goods). Whereas the industrialist provided a real article for sale to people, the businessman was motivated only by a desire to make profits. There was thus a conflict between technology (production) and capitalism (business). Veblen advocated the elimination of the price system of distribution in favor of government direction of industrial production and distribution. More astute (if more cautious) in their economic views were Rexford Guy Tugwell and Raymond Moley, Professors of Political Science at Columbia University. More interested in practical reform and progress than in theory, they

RAYMOND MOLEY

had long advocated the encouragement of corporate growth as a means of rationalizing the economy, but under strict government regulation and control to insure against economic exploitation of workers and the public.

With the onset of the Depression and the emergence of crisis as the everyday condition of social and political life, the many streams of reform and progressive thinking began to merge in a search of growing desperation for the political machinery through which they could attempt to reform American society before more radical philosophies overthrew it. Since the Republican Party remained firmly in the grip of Hooverism, the Democratic Party seemed to offer the only possible outlet for their ideas (although some brooded over the possibilities of a third party). And as a political leader for that party, attention was increasingly focused on a very remarkable man—Franklin Delano Roosevelt, the Governor of New York.

Franklin D. Roosevelt was born on January 30, 1882, at Hyde Park, a small town on the Hudson River not far north of New

York City. He was born to wealth and into the older, comfortable Dutch-descended aristocracy whose pleasant mansions and broad acres had for centuries dominated the Hudson Valley. A Roosevelt had been present when stump-legged Pieter Stuyvesant surrendered Nieuw Amsterdam to the English in 1664, and the family had been living in the outskirts of history ever since. In 1882 cousin Theodore Roosevelt was already in the New York State Assembly on his short, quick way to political power. But while Theodore's side of the family were devout Republicans, Franklin's side had returned to the older Democratic faith just after the Civil War.

When Franklin was five years old he visited Washington with his parents. They were received by President Grover Cleveland (who had vainly tried to get Franklin's father, James, to accept an ambassadorship), and as they were leaving the White House, the careworn President patted Franklin's head and said, "My little man, I am making a strange wish for you. It is that you may never be President of the United States."

Until he was fourteen, Franklin was educated by private tutors. Summers were often spent in Europe, although sometimes at Campobello Island off the coast of New Brunswick, Canada. In 1896 he was sent to Groton, a recently established private school for the sons of wealthy families. There he studied classics under the supervision of the strict rector, Endicott Peabody, and the harsh discipline of a school organized on the English model. Peabody imbued his boys with the ideal of Christian gentlemanliness. Because they were rich was all the more reason for them to discipline themselves and seek to serve humanity. Although he was somewhat lonely at Groton (unlike the other boys, he had never gone to a regular school before), Franklin did passably well, was manager of the school baseball team, won the Latin and Punctuality prizes, was a vigorous member of the Debating Society ("Resolved: The United States Ought to Annex the Hawaiian Islands"), and eventually made a few lasting friendships.

He entered Harvard in the fall of 1900, but the gaiety of that freshman autumn was darkened by the death of his father in

December. His seriousness (Rector Peabody had done his work well) earned him the reputation of being too intellectual among the boys of his own background; girls found him somewhat stiff and prudish. But by and large he led a pleasant life at Harvard and did so well at his studies that he was able to take his A.B. degree in three years instead of the usual four. He returned for his fourth year mainly, it appears, in order to edit the Harvard undergraduate newspaper, *The Crimson*. During his Harvard years, Franklin was a member of the Harvard Republican Club, largely because cousin Teddy was now (Republican) President of the United States. It was also during his years at Harvard that Franklin fell in love with a very distant cousin, Anna Eleanor Roosevelt, nineteen years old, a willowy, graceful girl, very shy, very intelligent, with a strength of character she had developed during a lonely and somber childhood.

In the fall of 1904 Franklin entered Columbia University Law School in New York City, and on March 17, 1905, he married (over his dominating mother's quiet objections) Eleanor. President Theodore Roosevelt journeyed from Washington to give the bride away (her parents were dead), and remarked in his bluff way, "Well, Franklin, there's nothing like keeping the name in the family!" At Columbia, Franklin was a dutiful student, and in 1907 he passed the New York State Bar examinations. Then he took his bride on a belated honeymoon to Europe. In Paris, he later recalled, he met a fortune teller who predicted he would be President one day, but she didn't say whether of the United States or the Equitable Life Assurance Company. Returning to New York, Franklin and Eleanor set up house on East 36th Street and began having children; they were to have six (one died in infancy) over the next ten years. Franklin worked as a junior clerk in the law offices of Carter, Ledyard and Millburn, a Wall Street law firm. There one day, chatting with the other junior clerks, Franklin amazed them by revealing that he hoped to go into politics and one day become President of the United States.

His opportunity came in 1910. In that year the upstate Democratic organization invited him to run for the State Senate from

FRANKLIN D. ROOSEVELT

Dutchess County, in which the family home, Hyde Park, was situated. Despite the fact that this was traditionally Republican territory, the vigor, gaiety, and personal charm (and connections) of the young candidate won his neighbors' support—and the election, by about 1,000 votes. He moved his family to Albany (the state capital) and soon earned a reputation as a Progressive, especially through his willingness to fight Tammany Hall, the New York City Democratic machine. It was during his quarrel with Tammany that he told a *New York Times* interviewer, "Business must get out of politics. The people must make a stand against it."

It was during the years in Albany, too, that Franklin was able to pursue one of his prime interests, conservation of natural resources. With his family background of farming in the Hudson Valley, Roosevelt well understood the need for conservation, and was very well versed in all its facets, from soil conservation to erosion to flood control. In Albany he led the (successful) fight to establish a State Conservation Authority. Perhaps his interest

ELEANOR ROOSEVELT

in preserving the state's natural resources led him to an interest
in preserving its human resources. In any event, he soon sponsored progressive labor legislation and won the political support
of state labor organizations. By this time, too, Eleanor Roosevelt
had become acquainted with the social welfare work of Lillian
Wald, and she was able to direct her husband's attention to the
desperate plight of poor people.

In 1911, Roosevelt (though not a delegate) attended the National Democratic Convention and campaigned for the nomination of Woodrow Wilson. Then, facing an election campaign of
his own, he returned to New York and promptly fell ill of typhoid
fever. Faced by opposition from Tammany Hall Democrats and
a strong Republican candidate in Dutchess County, it seemed
that Roosevelt's political career might come to an end. But into
the breach stepped a small, ugly, warm-hearted, cynical and idealistic (both at once) newspaperman named Louis McHenry
Howe. He had known and admired Roosevelt in Albany. Now,
with his wide experience in politics and his shrewd ability to or-

ganize a campaign, he became Roosevelt's political mentor and, incidentally, won the Dutchess County election handily in spite of having to represent an absentee candidate. From the very first, Howe seems to have made up his mind that Franklin was one day going to be President of the United States. All his devoted energies were to be bent towards making that dream come true.

But Roosevelt was not to stay long in the New York State Senate. When Woodrow Wilson was inaugurated President in 1912, he invited his enthusiastic supporter from Dutchess County to be Assistant Secretary of the Navy (a post once held by cousin Teddy). Roosevelt eagerly accepted and devoted himself during the next few years, under his chief, Josephus Daniels, the Navy Secretary, to building up America's fleets for a struggle which many felt was sure to come in an increasingly explosive world. His special responsibility was to supervise naval construction. This brought him into prolonged contact with businessmen and labor representatives. Though eminently successful in his dealings with labor (there was not a single strike in Navy shipyards during his time with the Navy Department), he soon found that he had to be wary of the sharp practices of steel companies. He might well have begun to wonder then whether giant private enterprises would ever willingly subordinate their interests to the public welfare.

In 1915, after a brief and unsuccessful attempt to win a Senate seat from New York in which he was defeated by the Tammany machine, Roosevelt made his peace with the New York City bosses and endorsed his old friend Al Smith for sheriff. Smith was a Tammany man, but by now Roosevelt realized that although the big-city machine might be corrupt, it was close to, and responsive to, the needs of the city's poor, in its own way. Years later, discussing Big Tim Sullivan, the Tammany leader, he could say, "Poor old Tim Sullivan never understood about modern politics, but he was right about the human heart."

The opening of World War I in 1914 had converted the Assistant Secretary of the Navy into a fireball of activity. He was an open advocate of the highest state of preparedness and, as time wore on, of American intervention to aid the Allies. When war eventually came, Roosevelt led the fight for the daring project of mining the North Sea against German U-boats. The North Sea mine barrage, when it was finally laid, proved highly effective against the undersea raiders. He attempted to resign and join the Army during 1918, but his work in Washington had become so necessary that his resignation was refused. But he did manage to wangle a trip to the front on inspection. He returned with double pneumonia and a deep impression of the horror of war. Later he and Eleanor accompanied Wilson to Paris. Their hopes for world order rose with Wilson's League of Nations in 1919 and faded with the disillusionments of 1919.

But Roosevelt's disillusionment did not weaken his commitment to his own ideals. When, in 1920, the Commandant of the Boston Navy Yard discharged some workers because of their political beliefs (at the height of Attorney General Palmer's Red scare), Roosevelt wrote to him: "Now, my dear Admiral, neither you nor I can fire a man because he happens to be a Socialist." The workers were reinstated.

Although he did not actively seek it, the Democratic convention of 1920 acclaimed him as candidate for Vice President (the Presidential candidate was James M. Cox) against Harding. No one expected the Democrats to win that year, and despite a vigorous campaign they went down to predictable defeat. But Roosevelt, campaigning for the first time through the entire country, made political friends and contacts which were to stand him in good stead later. After the defeat he returned to New York City to accept another Vice Presidency, that of the Fidelity and Deposit Company of Maryland. Then, in August, 1921, Roosevelt took his family on vacation to the favorite summer refuge, Campobello. On August 10, as they were sailing near the island, Roosevelt and the children noticed that a forest fire had broken out. Quickly beaching their boat they raced ashore and beat out the flames. Then, smoke begrimed and weary they plunged into the cold waters of the bay for a quick swim. When they returned home, Roosevelt suddenly felt himself exhausted and went to

LOUIS HOWE

bed. The next day he was running a fever, and he noticed that he had no feeling in his left leg. Soon his right leg was numb, too. A doctor was hastily summoned who diagnosed acute poliomyelitis, the dreaded "infantile (in children) paralysis." Quickly rushed back to New York's Presbyterian Hospital, Roosevelt was told by specialists that he might never sit up again, let alone walk.

Franklin D. Roosevelt was 39 years old when he was struck down by polio. His had been a vigorous athletic life until then, and one full of the highest promise. Now, apparently all that was finished. He would live out his days as an invalid. But Roosevelt had made a decision—perhaps the most important decision of his life—that he was not going to be defeated by polio. Although there was in those days no cure for the disease and only primitive treatment for its crippling results, he determined on a program of incessant and rigorous exercise to regain control of the muscles in his legs.

It was a long, slow, and painful struggle. It took months to learn to use crutches, and to crawl when the crutches slipped.

After a while, there were to be heavy iron leg braces, which, with the aid of a cane or someone's arm, permitted him to walk slowly and with tremendous effort. Over the years the muscles in his legs did improve, but despite his utmost exertions Roosevelt would never again walk alone unaided. Yet he indulged in no self-pity. "Since the beginning," Louis Howe observed, "I do not remember one complaint, one objection to the terrific discipline which he imposed upon himself." Roosevelt discovered that swimming was the best exercise for his condition because the water removed weight from his legs. And during the summer of 1924, hearing of the supposed therapeutic value of the natural springs at a run-down health resort in Warm Springs, Georgia, he decided to give them a try. The reports were correct; the spring-fed pool had a natural temperature of 89 degrees, and unusual buoyancy. It was, Roosevelt thought, ideal for exercising paralyzed muscles. Soon there were newspaper stories about the former Assistant Secretary of the Navy "swimming himself back to health." Other paralytics began to flock down to Warm Springs. There were no doctors available in those early days, but Roosevelt himself supervised activities. As more patients arrived, he brought in medical experts. In 1927 he purchased the springs and set up the Warm Springs Foundation as a non-profit center for the treatment of polio victims. The treatment there had helped him tremendously and was now to help thousands of others.

During the twenties, perhaps catching some of the enthusiasm for speculative business ventures, Roosevelt toyed with various money-making schemes. They ranged from establishing dirigible air lines in the United States to cornering the lobster market. But politics remained his first love. The normally shy and awkward Eleanor now transformed herself into an active and extremely able reporter and public speaker. She plunged into all sorts of activities, spoke (under Louis Howe's good-humored guidance) before women's organizations, welfare groups, and political meetings, and reported what she had learned in accurate and minute detail to her husband. Roosevelt himself carried on a large correspondence with Democratic Party leaders throughout the country, and the main theme of his letters to them was that the Democratic Party had to adopt liberal and progressive policies if it ever again hoped to win the White House. When, in 1924, Governor Al Smith of New York decided to try for the Democratic Presidential nomination, he made Roosevelt his campaign manager. That was a battle both men lost; John W. Davis became the Democratic candidate who was subsequently swamped by Coolidge. But the fight for Smith's nomination re-established Roosevelt as a national Democratic Party leader.

In 1928 Al Smith won the Democratic nomination, with Roosevelt acting as his floor manager at the national convention and making the speech which nominated him. In the subsequent campaign, Smith was to lose to Herbert Hoover—partly, at least, because Smith was a Roman Catholic. Roosevelt grew particularly angry over the whispering campaign started against Smith by various religious bigots. Hostility to a man because he was a Catholic, Roosevelt wrote, "makes my blood boil, as a Protestant of a long line of wholly Protestant ancestry."

But while Smith waged his losing national campaign, he persuaded Roosevelt to run for Governor of New York. At first reluctant (becoming Governor would seriously cut down on his visits to Warm Springs where he felt he was making remarkable progress), Roosevelt finally accepted and waged a vigorous campaign. Even though Smith lost nationally (and did not even carry his home state, New York, against Hoover) Roosevelt was elected.

Returning to Albany, where his political career had started years before, Roosevelt plunged with characteristic energy into his new responsibilities. He appointed social welfare worker Frances Perkins as Industrial Commissioner, and an old friend (and Hyde Park neighbor) Henry Morgenthau, Jr., as Chairman of the State Agricultural Advisory Commission. Louis Howe remained, of course, as chief political advisor. Despite the conservative atmosphere of 1928 and 1929, Roosevelt embarked on a progressive program for New York State. He continued Al Smith's fight to establish public power development on the Saint

HARRY L. HOPKINS

Lawrence River, waged an effective campaign for conservation of the state's natural resources, and pressed for the enactment of progressive state labor laws. As the country slipped into depression after the Wall Street Crash of 1929, Roosevelt, almost alone among state governors, gave urgent attention to the problems of unemployment and relief. In 1931, as local relief agencies throughout New York were being submerged by the flood of jobless and hungry people, Roosevelt established a New York State Temporary Emergency Relief Administration. As director of this new agency he appointed an energetic young social worker from New York City, Harry L. Hopkins. Roosevelt fought, too, for the establishment of unemployment insurance in New York and for the concept of economic planning to avoid the root causes of depression. His backing of such measures did not grow out of dogmatic belief in doctrine but out of humanitarian impulses. When conservative economists threw up their hands and suggested that the Depression would simply have to "work itself out," Roosevelt would reply scornfully, "People aren't cattle, you know!" In 1930, Roosevelt was re-elected Governor of New York by a margin of 750,000 votes, the largest plurality in the history of the state. Two years later he seemed a sure choice for the Democratic Presidential nomination.

But before reaching for this highest prize, Roosevelt felt the need of learning more about economics, of developing new programs with which to fight depression. To help him he enlisted the support of various experts, mostly from universities. The first of the group, which was later to be nicknamed "the Brain Trust," was Professor Raymond Moley, political scientist from Columbia University. Moley later brought along Professor Rexford Guy Tugwell, a Columbia economist. Later Professor Adolf A. Berle, Jr., an expert on credit and finance from Columbia Law School, joined the group. Through many a long evening of discussion and months of intensive study, these men educated Franklin Roosevelt in advanced economic and financial ideas. And he in turn educated them to the realities of political life. The group by no means felt it had all the answers, but it was anxious to learn. When the problem of agricultural surpluses proved too knotty for them, for example, Tugwell was sent West to interview Henry A. Wallace of Iowa, and learned of a plan for government control of crops which farmers themselves would support.

As the Democratic National Convention of 1932 approached, the Roosevelt team went vigorously and expertly to work to win him the Presidential nomination. Louis Howe now shared political responsibility with a big, bluff, expert professional politician from New York, James A. Farley. At the Convention in Chicago in June, the Roosevelt forces swept all before them and secured the nomination for their Governor. John Nance Garner was nominated for the Vice Presidency. Roosevelt, well aware of the crisis of despair into which the nation was plunged, decided not to wait for formal notification of his nomination in Albany. Instead, once again breaking precedent, he flew to Chicago to address the Convention in person. His presence seemed to electrify the delegates. Here was the man who had won his own harsh battle against fate; the man whose infectiously jaunty smile and confident voice seemed to challenge fear itself and to banish despair. To a wildly cheering audience, Roosevelt declared, "I pledge you, I pledge myself, to a new deal for the American people." The band struck up the Roosevelt campaign song, "Happy Days Are Here Again!", and for a moment in Chicago that summer, the pall of gloom lifted from American hearts.

There was never any real question as to who would win the Presidential election. In the Depression year of 1932 probably any Democrat would have won. Hoover's Republicans, who had, quite naturally and in the best political tradition, claimed all the credit for the boom years, now had to shoulder (somewhat unfairly) all the blame for the bust. Furthermore, the Republicans quickly lost their more progressive supporters. Senators Bob La Follette of Wisconsin, George Norris of Nebraska, Bronson Cutting of New Mexico, and Hiram Johnson of California led a large-scale defection to Democratic ranks in 1932. And despite Roosevelt's talk of a "new deal" which would, presumably, finally dethrone business from its dominant position on the political scene, some notable business leaders backed him. They included Vincent Astor, William Randolph Hearst, Pierre S. DuPont, James W. Gerard, Joseph P. Kennedy, and others.

Roosevelt was advised by conservative Democrats that since his election was all but certain, he should risk losing no votes by making precise statements of what he proposed to do which might invite effective Republican attack. And it is true that during the campaign of 1932, FDR (the newspapers were quick to dub him by his initials) did not spell out his subsequent plans in any detail. But he certainly let the people know the directions his administration would take. In Topeka, Kansas, he called for an agricultural allotment plan that foreshadowed government control of farm surpluses; in Portland, Oregon, he called for government regulation of public utilities and government construction and control of various dam and power developments; in San Francisco he urged that government would now have to intervene in the world of giant corporations in order to make sure the public interest was not overlooked; in Sioux City, Iowa, he called for a new and more liberal tariff policy. And always he insisted that the federal government must assume responsibility for the relief of the starving and homeless. This, of course, implied heavy new federal taxes—or an unbalanced budget. Only on this issue did Roosevelt hedge. In Pittsburgh he called for government retrenchment and a balanced budget, although he knew quite well that such a policy was incompatible with his entire program.

Everywhere the people came to see FDR in huge throngs. They gathered at lonely little railroad crossings in the West just to catch a glimpse of the campaign train; they lined the streets of towns and cities in dense masses; they filled to overflowing the public stadiums and arenas where he spoke. Their faces were grave at first, their eyes searching with quiet intensity the face of the man who might just possibly supply a few answers to agonizing questions. But soon they would begin to smile, to catch the jaunty enthusiasm behind the up-tilted cigarette holder, the infectious grin, the voice (it seemed made for radio) which could so well express stern disapproval (of heartless corporations), poke satiric jibes (at humorless Republicans), and speak warmly and directly to people in the language of hope. For above all, the impression made by FDR was one of confidence—confidence in the people, confidence in the future. Perhaps his listeners did not always understand the full implications of the new programs he was proposing, but they understood that he promised vigorous leadership, a change, something new—and a renewal of faith in America itself.

Hoover fought a losing campaign with energy and increasing bitterness. He sensed and, as he traveled through the country, saw direct evidence that the people hated him. He felt (not without reason) that he did not deserve this hatred from the nation he had served for so many years. In Des Moines, Iowa, he was greeted by marching farmers bearing banners reading: "IN HOOVER WE TRUSTED; NOW WE ARE BUSTED." In Detroit silent people lined his route with such signs as "DOWN WITH HOOVER." Jeers and catcalls greeted the President of the United States in many a town and city. Nor did Hoover offer anything new. He insisted continuously on high tariffs, no government "interference" in the economic or social spheres, and a balanced budget. Increasingly he began to accuse the Democrats of waging a revolutionary campaign to change the very nature of the American government. In New York he said, "This election . . . means deciding the direction our Nation will take over a century to come." Nor was he far wrong in that statement. When, in St. Paul, he told an audience, "Thank God we still have a government in Washington that knows how to deal with the mob," angry murmurs began to roll up from the crowd in front of him (thinking, no doubt, of the fate of the Bonus Army). The Secret Service men guarding Hoover became alarmed. The President lost his place in the speech he was giving, nearly collapsed, and at last retreated from the auditorium badly shaken.

In November the people spoke. Roosevelt received 22,822,000 votes against Hoover's 15,762,000 and carried every state in the Union except six. If this was not an overwhelming victory for the still obscure policies of the New Deal, it was certainly a tremendous repudiation of Hoover's Old Deal. In Hyde Park, listening to the election returns, Louis Howe brought forth a bottle of sherry he had put aside twenty years before, not to be opened until Roosevelt was elected President. Raising his glass he quietly proposed a toast, "To the next President of the United States!"

But in 1932, a new President was not inaugurated until March 4 of the following year (a lapse of time which would subsequently be shortened by amendment of the Constitution). And as the nation waited, Depression despair and desperation increased. The unemployment figure now hovered around 15,000,000. Out West farmers were using shotguns and nooses to prevent foreclosures of mortgages. As the new year of 1933 opened, banks throughout the country were failing with alarming frequency. The sight of long lines of hopeful depositors waiting outside bank doors to withdraw their life's savings before the banks had no more money to give them became familiar.

During the interim, President Hoover invited Roosevelt to

cooperate in a number of matters. But discussions soon revealed that Hoover was simply trying to pre-commit the new President-elect to his old policies, and this Roosevelt rejected. Hoover's bitterness grew as Inauguration Day approached.

On February 15, 1933, Roosevelt, driving through Miami, Florida, with Chicago's Mayor Anton Cermak, was the victim of an assassination attempt. An unemployed bricklayer named Joe Zangara emptied his revolver at the President-elect ("I have always hated the rich and powerful . . . I hate all Presidents . . . ," Zangara said) but succeeded only in killing Mayor Cermak. The nation was alarmed, but also heartened by the reports of Roosevelt's calm courage during and after the event.

Certainly the people needed heartening. The day before the assassination attempt Michigan's governor was forced to declare a bank moratorium. That is, by executive decree he closed all the banks in his state to save them from the panic which swept through people rushing to withdraw their deposits before their money vanished. Other state governors began to declare bank moratoriums of their own. Banks which had unwisely invested in shaky bonds and mortgages and whose finances had been depleted by unethical management could no longer pay out the money people had placed in them for savings or checking accounts. Not only individuals, but corporations and foreign depositors and investors began to withdraw money as fast as they could. Bank after bank was forced to close its doors. By March 3, 1933, even the great New York and Chicago banks were collapsing, and the governors of twelve states declared moratoriums. The American financial system had ceased to function; there was no more money with which to buy anything or to pay anyone. In Washington, on March 4, the last day of his term of office, a haggard and care-worn Herbert Hoover remarked, "We are at the end of our string. There is nothing more we can do."

March 4 was Inauguration Day. It was a cloudy day in Washington as the out-going President and President-elect Franklin D. Roosevelt drove together down Pennsylvania Avenue to the inauguration stand outside the Capitol building. Soldiers with mounted machine guns faced the gathered crowds along the route, as if expecting a revolutionary outburst at any moment. There was only faint applause from the spectators. Hoover's attitude was one of glum bitterness as the car drove slowly through the city he was now leaving. Roosevelt smiled and waved his hat at the crowds, but it was apparent that the atmosphere was more one of tension than enthusiasm.

At last the ride was over. As the Marine band played "Hail to the Chief," Roosevelt walked slowly up the red carpet (his legs locked in heavy steel braces, leaning on the arm of his son James) to where Charles Evans Hughes, Chief Justice of the United States, awaited to administer the Oath of Office. In the crowd of spectators could be seen Mrs. Woodrow Wilson, waving a handkerchief; old Josephus Daniels, crying, pounding his cane vigorously; and many, many of the men and women who had helped to shape the career and life of the new President.

After repeating the oath (his hand resting on the family Bible opened to that passage of First Corinthians: "And now abideth faith, hope, charity, these three; but the greatest of these *is* charity"), Franklin D. Roosevelt addressed the nation for the first time as President. Across the country millions of people clustered around their radios as they heard a vigorous voice proclaim: "Let me assert my firm belief that the only thing we have to fear is fear itself—nameless, unreasoning, unjustified terror which paralyzes needed efforts to convert retreat into advance . . . This Nation asks for action, and action now . . . the people of the United States have not failed. In their need they have registered a mandate that they want vigorous action . . . They have made me the present instrument of their wishes. In the spirit of the gift I take it."

The Marine Corps bugles sounded as the inaugural parade got underway. Suddenly, the packed throngs in Washington were cheering. A voice of determination and confidence had lifted people beyond their despair. Terrible problems remained to be solved; hard times would not vanish overnight, but hope was abroad in the land once more.

five The Hundred Days— and a Day

In the darkness with a great bundle of grief
  the people march
In the night, and overhead a shovel of stars for
  keeps, the people march:
                    "Where to? what next?"
                    Carl Sandburg

... there is nothing to do but meet every day's
troubles as they come. What terrible decisions we'll
have to make! and sometimes we'll be wrong!
                    Franklin D. Roosevelt

THE IMPORTANT, the urgent thing to do was to make decisions.
To help him make them the new President had already chosen
his Cabinet; its members were sworn in together at the White
House on March 4, 1933. For Secretary of State Roosevelt had
chosen the reform-minded Congressman from Tennessee, Cordell Hull; Harold Ickes, the tough Progressive, became Secretary
of the Interior; William Woodin, a relatively liberal businessman, was sworn in as Secretary of the Treasury; Henry A. Wallace, the Iowa farmer-editor-plant geneticist, long-time supporter
of government regulation of agriculture, became Secretary of
Agriculture; social worker and industrial relations expert Frances
Perkins (the first woman Cabinet member) was Secretary of

Labor; Homer Cummings, Connecticut's radical attorney general, became Attorney General; James A. Farley, the shrewd and hearty New York professional politician, took over as Postmaster General; Wilsonian liberal Daniel C. Roper became Secretary of Commerce; Claude Swanson of Virginia was Secretary of the Navy; and George Dern, a progressive reformer from Utah, became Secretary of War. Roosevelt's "unofficial family," the Brain Trust, hovered for a moment in the background: Raymond Moley, Rexford Tugwell, Adolf Berle, Judge Sam Rosenman, his secretary Marguerite "Missy" LeHand, Marvin McIntyre, and the indispensable Louis Howe.

The most urgent matter before the new President was the nationwide collapse of the banking system. Not only the banks but also the New York Stock Exchange and the Chicago Grain Exchange were closed; the nation's financial heart had ceased to beat. Four hours after the inauguration FDR called in Secretary of the Treasury William Woodin and ordered him to prepare emergency legislation regulating the banks, and he gave him just five days in which to do it. The following day Roosevelt issued two Presidential proclamations. The first declared a national bank "holiday," shutting down those few banks which had not already collapsed; the second was an edict (based on half-forgotten Presidential powers stemming from a World War I Trading with the Enemy Act) forbidding the export of gold. These two measures bought time, a few days' time, in which to work out an entirely new national banking policy before the new session (a special session called by Roosevelt to meet the emergency) of Congress convened on March 9.

Under the tireless supervision of Secretary Woodin, a strange combination of individuals worked around the clock at the Treasury. They included Hoover's former Secretary of the Treasury, Ogden Mills, and his staff; New Dealers such as Raymond Moley (now an Assistant Secretary of State); economists from universities; and scores of worried, desperate bankers. Moley recalled: "We had forgotten to be Republicans or Democrats. We were just a bunch of men trying to save the banking system."

The fact that they were trying to save the banking system rather than to replace it represented a key decision already made by Roosevelt. There were many during those frantic days, including Senators Robert La Follette, Bronson Cutting, and Edward Costigan, as well as brain-truster Rexford Tugwell (now an Assistant Secretary of Agriculture), who thought this a fine opportunity to nationalize the banks. Many such programs were offered, including one whereby the nation's post offices would take over the savings and checking functions of banks. Others urged that the government issue scrip from central clearing houses to replace currency. Nor would a move to nationalize the entire banking system have met with much public opposition. During his last weeks in office, President Hoover had asked Congress to investigate the Stock Exchange. Hoover had expected that the investigation (conducted by Senator Duncan Fletcher of Florida, but really run by former New York County Assistant District Attorney Ferdinand Pecora) would prove that financial manipulation by certain Wall Street brokers had brought about the Crash and prevented recovery. But the Pecora investigation turned up more and more evidence of widespread stupidity and criminality among the members of the entire financial community. Charles Mitchell of the National City Bank was later to be indicted for embezzlement; A. H. Wiggin of the Chase National Bank, Clarence Dillon, Winthrop Aldrich, and Stock Exchange President Richard Whitney testified to unethical practices among the money kings. Pecora showed how J. P. Morgan and his partners had evaded paying their income taxes for years. Then he went on to uncover the Morgan practice of selling stocks at greatly reduced prices (below what the public would have to pay) to a "preferred list" of customers including such notables as General John J. Pershing, Charles Lindbergh, Calvin Coolidge, Supreme Court Justice Owen J. Roberts, Democratic "elder statesman" Bernard Baruch, and former Secretary of War Newton D. Baker. As the New York Times pointed out, by accepting such unethical favors from Morgan, many of the nation's public leaders had placed themselves under obligation to him.

Referring to the "preferred list," Republican Governor Alfred M. Landon of Kansas declared, "It is nothing more nor less than bribery." Many of the most sensational exposures of the Pecora investigation would come later, but by early March, 1933, enough had been revealed for the American people to recoil indignantly from the evidence of chicanery, greed, and simple-mindedness among the nation's largest bankers. And the failure of the banks, which had wiped out untold millions in life savings, seemed a final indictment on the entire private banking system. Roosevelt himself had declared in his inaugural address that ". . . the rulers of the exchange of mankind's goods have failed through their own stubbornness and their own incompetence, have admitted their failure, and have abdicated . . . The money changers have fled from their high seats in the temple of our civilization."

And yet even with a favorable opportunity, Roosevelt refused to pull the seats finally and completely out from under the money changers. And this was, for those able to see, the first sign that he did not intend to preside over a socialization of the United States. Rather, he was determined to preserve capitalism from its own errors, to discipline the system, if necessary, but not to fundamentally change it.

As Congress convened on March 9, an exhausted William Woodin was able to send it a draft of the new banking act with some last-minute changes scribbled into it by pencil. Even while the Speaker of the House read the bill, voices were heard shouting, "Vote! Vote!" The measure was passed by acclamation and rushed over to the Senate. There it passed (over the objections of certain Progressives who found the bill too conservative) by a vote of 73 to 7 a few hours later, and was signed into law by Roosevelt at 8:30 that same evening. In effect, the new banking law extended government assistance to private banks, gave the President complete control over gold shipments, penalized hoarding of gold, authorized the government to issue new currency through the Federal Reserve Banks (federal reserve notes), placed failed banks into government receivership, and arranged for the orderly reopening of those banks with sufficient funds left in their vaults. It was a bill which met with the approval of bankers and even of the most conservative members of Hoover's old administration.

Meanwhile the country had responded to the national bank holiday as if it were just that—a holiday. Ingenious means had been devised to keep financial wheels turning on a small scale. In the North and Northwest, some people used Canadian money; in the Southwest, Mexican pesos. Dance halls, speakeasies, department stores, grocery stores, and hotels extended credit. The final closing of the banks had seemed to put a period to the Depression—it could never get worse than this, only better. On Sunday, March 12, people across the country gathered around their radios to hear the first of Franklin Roosevelt's "fireside chats." He adopted the name, as he later explained, because he wanted these radio talks to have the friendly air and informality of a neighborly discussion such as might take place before the hearth of a family home. The President told his audience that the banks were now secure, that it was safe to deposit money in them. And so magnetic was his radio personality, so widespread was public trust in the man himself, that when on the following day, Monday, March 13, the banks reopened their doors, deposits actually exceeded withdrawals. The crisis of money seemed to be over. "Capitalism," Raymond Moley observed, "was saved in eight days."

Even before the fireside chat, Roosevelt had sent an economy bill to Congress. Influenced by the conservative views of Budget Director Lewis Douglas, and perhaps by the instinctive fiscal conservatism of his landed-aristocratic background, Roosevelt overrode the objections of his Brain Trust and asked Congress to reduce veterans' pensions by $400 million and federal government employees' salaries by $100 million. Progressive and liberal Senators were aghast at these proposals. Not only were they politically explosive (all those veterans' votes!), but they removed money from circulation just at the time when many felt the need of pouring more money into the stricken economy. Nevertheless, Congress obediently passed the economy measure.

More popular with Congress was the message Roosevelt sent on March 13. This called for amendment of the Volstead Act to permit the manufacture and sale of beer. Congress had already (in February, 1933) voted to repeal the Eighteenth (Prohibition) Amendment. The Twenty-first (Repeal) Amendment was awaiting only the necessary approval of thirty-six states to become law. But while waiting for whiskey, the nation would have beer. Over the objections of the few die-hard "dry" Congressmen, Representatives and Senators added wine to beer just for good measure and chanted "Vote—vote—we want beer!" On April 7, 1933, beer was again legal in America. In New York City six heavy brewery horses pulled a bright red beer wagon up to the Empire State Building and presented Al Smith with a case of lager. In the "beer cities," St. Louis and Milwaukee, thousands thronged the streets singing "Sweet Adeline." Happy days were really here again, it seemed.

And it was true, as Walter Lippmann observed, that in barely two weeks Roosevelt had achieved a lifting of morale comparable to that in the Battle of the Marne in the First World War. Everywhere people felt the current of change, of hope. President Charles Edison of the Thomas A. Edison Company in Orange, New Jersey, marched into his factory and posted a notice that read:

President Roosevelt has done his part: now you do something.

Buy something—buy anything, anywhere; paint your kitchen, send a telegram, give a party, get a car, pay a bill, rent a flat, fix your roof, get a haircut, see a show, build a house, take a trip, sing a song, get married.

It does not matter what you do—but get going and keep going. This old world is starting to move!

The advice may have seemed slightly gratuitous to the underpaid employees of Mr. Edison, but there was little doubt that businessmen, at any rate, were pleased with Roosevelt's program so far. But that New Deal they feared had not been canceled, and now it descended in a rush of laws and proposals.

On March 16, Roosevelt sent a farm message to Congress. The

work of many Brain Trusters, as well as Secretary of Agriculture Henry Wallace and important farm leaders from all over the country, the Agricultural Adjustment Act proposed a variety of means whereby farm prices could be supported by the government. Primary among these was a system whereby the federal government would pay farmers to remove fields from cultivation (thereby cutting down the immense yearly farm surpluses and indirectly raising prices). The payments would be financed, at least partly, from a tax on food-processing industries, such as canners and meat packers. Another provision of the bill allowed the President, at his discretion, to sell surplus farm products abroad for whatever price they would bring. The administration of the farm program, though centered in Washington, was to be handled through local organizations, county agents, and land-grant colleges. Progressive Senators thought the plan did not go far enough, and conservatives were shocked by it. Food processors complained bitterly of the proposed tax on their corporations. Nevertheless, Congress swallowed the measure on May 12, but not before first amending it.

For generations, Progressives had insisted that the solution to the farmers' problems lay in devaluation of the dollar. A dollar based on gold was simply too expensive for farmers; one based on silver would be cheaper, would permit farmers to pay off their debts in easier-to-earn dollars. "Free silver" had been the rallying cry of farmers since the days of William Jennings Bryan. Now the Senate, over Roosevelt's objections, attached to the AAA bill an amendment sponsored by Oklahoma Senator Elmer Thomas, authorizing the President to devalue the dollar by restoring silver as a monetary unit by printing greenbacks or altering the gold content of the dollar. Roosevelt accepted the amendment because there was little else he could do, and he preferred being given a choice of policies to a rigid law. On April 19, 1933, Roosevelt announced to newsmen that the United States was off the gold standard.

The AAA was further enhanced in June by the establishment of the Farm Credit Administration (under Henry Morgenthau,

headliners

Intimate Moments With Gold Coast Folk

Facing pages, *Boston Sunday Post Pictorial*, February 14, 1937.

Uncensored Views of Share-Croppers' Misery

POVERTY'S CHILDREN—Burlap bags serve as clothes for these share-cropper's children, in North Carolina. It is the aim of the Resettlement Administration at Washington to better these families to better land, their present fields being almost ruined by the one crop—King Cotton.

AN ARKANSAS JEETER LESTER—Those who have seen the play "Tobacco Road," will better understand the environment in which this Arkansas share-cropper lives. His home, in an official government photo, is shown above, and he represents an extreme, but not a rare degree of poverty.

His share of the meagre crop of cotton he raises on worn-out land keeps him and his family alive, but gives them none for clothes, good food, or for repairs to the shack which he feels may be taken from him tomorrow.

EIR HOME—AND WHAT A HOME!—The plight of the Southern share-croppers these people, who grow cotton on shares, is largely the result of a single crop system, which not the end of trouble, for lands they till to be certainties in a single market. ... a typical family in Arkansas, the children wearing sacks made into garments. The mother, pucked ... and despair, wears a man's cracked shoes. The well-worn broom and cleanliness of the crude ... would seem to indicate that there place is not due to shiftlessness. The children, good stock, would ... with proper opportunity. The family little lass he could be a Cinderella in any place.

BLEAK DWELLINGS

A frequent sight is the cabin is a cotton, the porch packed with cotton, as at left. Cotton is everywhere, in the share-cropper, he must use his bedroll and provide for his family's needs. The ... of the crude scales family shows above the cotton. Cotton plants are almost touching the sides of the cabin.

At the right is the view ... ing share-cropper's home, and it is a good one, as many of them go. Cotton right at the door of a crumbling, leaky dwelling. The closeness, also but for a long time, isn't touched because bricks and mortar, and the owner here can hardly buy his family "back luck and overalls" for their poor land. A great part of the Resettlement Administration's work is to reach these people to rotate crops, raise more of their own food, and raise enough to be let to travels money.

Chicago, July 2, 1932. Governor Franklin D. Roosevelt and his family arrived here today by airplane. Breaking tradition, the New York Governor has flown to the Democratic National Convention to make his speech accepting the Presidential nomination immediately and in person.

Miami, Feb. 16, 1933. Mayor Anton Cermak of Chicago was fatally shot here today. Police say the assassin was really trying to kill President-elect Franklin D. Roosevelt as he sat next to Cermak in a limousine.

Los Angeles, Dec. 17, 1934. Monte Blue, Will Rogers, Jackie Cooper and Jimmy Durante are among the galaxy of stars who will perform tonight at the Shrine Auditorium. They're donating their salaries to charity.

Chicago, Dec. 20, 1934. Public Enemy Number One, John Dillinger, has been killed by police and FBI agents outside a local movie theater.

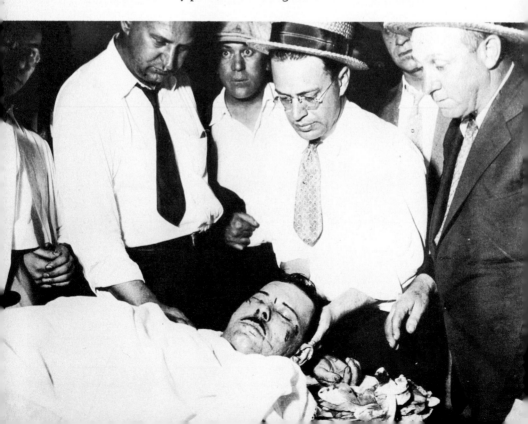

Flemington, N.J., Jan. 8, 1935. Bruno Richard Hauptmann, accused of having kidnapped and then murdered Charles Lindbergh's infant son in 1932, faces trial here today. Hauptmann denies the charges.

Atlantic City, Oct. 15, 1935. AFL President William Green fought here today to keep control of his organization. He is being opposed by a group of militants, led by mineworker boss John L. Lewis, who demand large-scale industrial unionization.

Abilene, Kansas, Aug. 28, 1936. This charming young lady is sporting a sunflower hat, national campaign symbol of Republican Alf Landon. *The Literary Digest* magazine predicts Landon of Kansas will defeat President Roosevelt by a record vote.

New York, Feb. 20, 1936. New York City Mayor Fiorello H. LaGuardia
affixes his signature to the agreement which will bring peace to New
York's garment industry. Watching him sign the new labor pact are
(left) David Dubinsky, ILGWU President, and (right) Herman
Florsheimer, President of the Dress Manufacturers' Ass'n.

Hollywood, Jan 12, 1937. Ginger Rogers and Fred Astaire rehearse a
dance number from their new million-dollar musical *Follow The Fleet,*
soon to be released.

Detroit, May 10, 1937. Richard Frankensteen (right) and Walter Reuther, two CIO United Autoworkers organizers, were badly beaten here today by unknown assailants. The two labor leaders charge company guards with the crime.

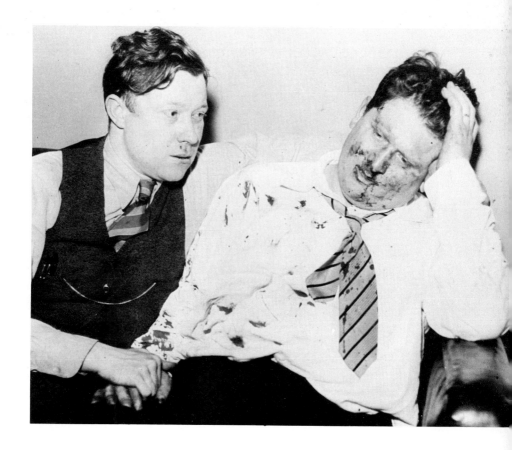

Crossville, Tenn., July 12, 1937. Mrs. Franklin D. Roosevelt addressed a crowd of relocated workers here today. The First Lady is touring the entire TVA area to explain the government's resettlement program.

St. Louis, Nov. 27, 1938. Trumpeter Louis Armstrong and singer Maxine Sullivan hit a few high notes as they prepare their new show which they hope to bring to New York next month.

Washington, March 4, 1939. Chief Justice Charles Evans Hughes leads his Supreme Court colleagues into the House of Representatives. Official ceremonies were held there today to mark the 150th anniversary of the first meeting of Congress under the Constitution.

Hollywood, Dec. 5, 1939. The movie version of John Steinbeck's *The Grapes of Wrath* will soon be released. Pictured here (left to right) are Eddie Quillan as Al; Dorris Bowdon as Rose of Sharron; John Carradine as the Preacher; and Henry Fonda as Tom Joad.

Jr.) which refinanced farm mortgages throughout the country, buying them away from banks and insurance companies, lowering interest charges, extending payments, and generally putting a stop to the flood of farm foreclosures. The farmer now had price supports (the fight over how these were to be established would go on for years), the prospect of plenty of greenbacks, and security on his land. After fifty years of struggle, the American farmer was becoming a first-class citizen.

FDR had for many years been a leader in the fight for conservation of natural resources. It was a problem he understood well. He also understood something of the anguish of the unemployed, especially young people, many of whom had taken to simply wandering the roads. It was his idea to establish a conservation corps which would help to preserve the nation's physical heritage and at the same time offer employment to many thousands of young people. But when he proposed a Civilian Conservation Corps to his Cabinet they responded by urging upon him a more comprehensive program which would provide relief for all the unemployed. On March 21, Roosevelt sent a message to Congress which proposed not only a Civilian Conservation Corps but also the granting of $500 million by the federal government to state relief organizations. Eight days later the CCC was law, and soon (by July, 1933) over 300,000 boys were off the roads and into CCC camps run by the United States Army and administered by the Labor Department. They set to work on such projects as land clearance, forestry, dam building, national park improvement, and land reclamation. In the process, many reclaimed themselves as well as the land. Many came from city slums, most were undernourished. In the forests and mountains of the West they hardened their muscles, grew tan and healthy, and, above all, felt that they were doing something really useful. Eventually, over 2.5 million boys were to pass through the CCC camps; almost none regretted it. Many felt as a Cleveland boy did who said, "I feel almost as if I owned that land. Some day when those trees I planted grow large I want to go back and look at them." Many millions of Americans in later years would be looking at those trees, vacationing in the national parks, farming the reclaimed land, enjoying the heritage preserved for them by the CCC.

Although the CCC was a popular measure, the grant of $500 million to state relief agencies provoked opposition in Congress among financial conservatives and those who still clung to the belief that helping the starving was a local responsibility. Nonetheless, Congress passed a bill on March 30, 1933, creating a Federal Emergency Relief Administration to distribute the $500 million. To head it, Roosevelt called in his former chief of New York State relief programs, Harry Hopkins. The thin, chain-smoking Hopkins proved to be a fireball of energy. Within two days after his arrival in Washington he had gathered a staff; within weeks he was descending on state governors and relief agencies, urging more efficiency, greater speed, more honesty— and disbursing federal money as fast as he could. Nevertheless, Hopkins understood very well that direct relief—handouts, whether state or federal—humiliated and demoralized those who received them. "It is probably going to undermine the independence of hundreds of thousands of families," he wrote in June, 1933. ". . . I look upon this as a great disaster and wish to handle it as such." Hopkins constantly searched for some way to dignify relief payments, but he was not to find his answer for several months.

On April 10, Roosevelt sent yet another message to Congress, this time asking for the fulfillment of an old Progressive dream: the establishment of a Tennessee Valley Authority. For many years, Congressional Progressives led by Senator George Norris of Nebraska had fought unsuccessfully for federal government operation of the Muscle Shoals electric and nitrogen development which had been built at public expense on the Tennessee River during World War I. Norris himself was chiefly interested in the cheap electric power government operation could provide to the farmers of the area. Others, especially Southern farm leaders, were interested by the prospect of manufacturing cheap fertilizer. Others saw a chance to prevent floods and stop soil

3517

erosion through careful control of the river itself. Roosevelt was excited by all these possibilities. Furthermore, he saw the various projects as part of a large-scale planning operation which would embrace the entire region, with many dams, fertilizer plants, soil control stations, even new towns and cities, planned and built for the poverty-stricken inhabitants of the Tennessee Valley. Private electric companies objected furiously. Although they found no profit in bringing electricity to the local farmers themselves and had no interest at all in the conservation or navigation aspects of the proposal, they feared that if the government itself went into the electric power business it would force down electricity rates. Furthermore, TVA might be the opening wedge in a federal drive to take over the entire public power sector. The fight over TVA would continue with increasing bitterness. But during the spring of 1933, there were few who cared to challenge the President's program. TVA was enacted into law on May 18.

Eight days later, largely because of the flagrant exposures resulting from Ferdinand Pecora's investigation of the bankers, Congress passed the so-called "Truth-in-Securities Act," which gave the Federal Trade Commission power to supervise the issuing of new securities—stocks and bonds—and required that each new stock be accompanied by a thorough statement as to the company's financial reliability and economic assets and prospects. Company directors would be criminally liable for misstatements. This measure represented a victory for the Wilsonian liberals in Congress and a victory for the concept of regulating business rather than coercing it or directing it.

June opened with a New Deal bill which made illegal the clauses of contracts, public or private, which required payment in gold—another step towards devaluation of the dollar or, as some feared, inflation. Contracts could now be paid with dollars which were worth less than they had been when the contract was first signed. This brought relief to debtors, big corporations as well as private parties. A more thoroughgoing and far-reaching relief for debt was provided on June 13 when the Home Owners' Loan Act appeared in Congress. By the terms of this bill, a Home

Owners' Loan Corporation was set up by the federal government to refinance home mortgages for those who had lost their homes as far back as 1930 and those who could not find mortgage money at the time. Within a short time one out of every ten American owners of mortgaged homes had received HOLC financing. The fear of foreclosure was lifted from millions of middle-class families; how real that fear had been is demonstrated by the appalling figure of 1,000 foreclosures *daily* in early 1933, before HOLC. The measure also boosted the real estate and construction industries.

On June 16, another banking law was debated in Congress and passed without opposition. This was the Glass-Steagal Banking Act (named after its sponsors, Senator Carter Glass of Virginia and Representative Henry Steagal of Alabama). The bill separated commercial from investment banking: henceforth a bank might undertake one activity or the other, not both. But, of much greater lasting importance, the act set up the Federal Deposit Insurance Corporation whereby the Federal Government insured the deposits of private citizens in banks up to the amount of $10,000. Much debated at the time, deposit insurance was to prove one of the most popular of the New Deal reforms; at a single stroke it ended the worries which had plagued small depositors since the beginning of the republic.

On the same day (June 16, 1933) Congress adopted the Farm Credit Act and the Railroad Coordination Act, both of which simplified credit activities and transportation problems within the framework of federal supervision.

But of all the measures of the "Hundred Days," none was more controversial, closer to Roosevelt's heart, or of greater significance than the National Industrial Recovery Act, adopted by Congress on June 15. The NIRA (soon abbreviated to NRA for National Recovery Administration) was the very core of the first New Deal program to deal with the Depression. It was intended as an experiment in business-government cooperation to achieve definite economic and social goals. The final law was the work of many men with differing ideas as to how best to deal with the nation's problems, and to a certain extent there was something in the NRA to please all of them (and something to irritate all of them). Business leaders had for some time been pleading with the Roosevelt administration to suspend enforcement of the Sherman Anti-Trust Act. They argued that only if large corporations were permitted to plan together for the future, set tradewide production standards and nationwide prices, could real recovery take place. New Dealers such as Rexford Tugwell, liberal Senators like LaFollette and New York's Robert Wagner, saw in such proposals a chance for the federal government to begin regulating business for the national good with the approval of businessmen. Secretary of Labor Frances Perkins and labor leaders such as John L. Lewis and Sidney Hillman saw in NRA an opportunity to win such advances as an end to child labor, minimum wages, and the forty-hour work week, for if industry was to be permitted to escape the anti-trust laws then industry would have to accept tradewide and nationwide fair-dealing with labor, too. In the meantime, many New Dealers, such as Secretary of the Interior Ickes, Henry Wallace, and Harry Hopkins, had been urging a gigantic program of federally sponsored and financed public works on the President. Aside from improving the public domain, these works would provide employment for millions of Americans, put large sums of money into circulation, and act as an indirect spur to business in the areas in which they were undertaken. The NRA then was to be a vehicle for relief, reform, and recovery. In the end, businessmen got government authorization to draw up "codes" of behavior, production, pricing, and fair competition practices for each industry; the New Deal regulators won their demand for government licensing of business; labor was guaranteed minimum wages, maximum hours, and the right to organize and bargain collectively; the advocates of Public Works were given $3.3 billion to get their program underway. The entire program was put under the supervision of fiery old General Hugh Johnson (although the Public Works section, organized as the Public Works Administration, was placed under the control of Interior Secretary Ickes).

GENERAL HUGH JOHNSON

This, then, was the "hundred days." When Congress adjourned on June 16, exactly one hundred days after the special session had opened, Roosevelt had steered fifteen major new laws and scores of minor ones to adoption. The New Deal had basically altered the American economic order, had determined new directions for American democracy (just as Herbert Hoover had fearfully predicted) for decades to come, and had laid foundations for social changes more far-reaching than any man could have predicted in 1933. Yet the New Deal had not overturned the American system. It had, instead, brought first aid to the American capitalist system, first aid to millions of unemployed people, first aid to the American spirit. But only time would tell if it had effected any permanent cures.

The hundred-day special session of Congress was an exciting period; every day seemed to be punctuated by a new law, a new idea in government. But in some ways none of these days was as significant as a day in May when no new law was passed. It was a day which saw assemble in Washington a new Bonus Expeditionary Force. Although not so big as the one routed by General MacArthur, it was still several thousand strong. And there were the same despairing, gaunt faces, the same ragged hopes, the same undernourished desperations which had so frightened President Hoover. But instead of shacks and shanties on Anacostia Flats, the new BEF found itself housed in an Army camp and fed three solid meals a day. The U.S. Navy band played for the veterans, and Army doctors ministered to their ills. Their leaders were granted an immediate conference with the President, and on a rainy day not long afterwards Louis Howe and Mrs. Eleanor Roosevelt visited the veterans' camp. Mrs. Roosevelt waded through ankle-deep mud to meet and talk to the veterans and wound up leading them in singing "There's a Long, Long Trail A-winding." As one veteran remarked, "Hoover sent the Army, Roosevelt sent his wife." Most of the members of the second BEF were enrolled in the Civilian Conservation Corps; the others went home content in the knowledge that there was someone in the White House who cared about them. And this was the feeling prevalent throughout America: the President cared; the wheels of government were turning again; the "forgotten man" was not forgotten after all. The feeling was based, finally, on intuitive faith, for none of the New Deal measures had yet had time to effect any basic changes. But faith moves mountains, sometimes. And the faith in Roosevelt that the American people developed, which was really a renewal of faith in themselves, was to prove the most lasting, if intangible, victory of the hundred-days war.

six The First New Deal

It happens, fortunately it seems to me,
that the Biblical record is heavily loaded
on the side of the Progressive Independents.
Henry A. Wallace

This is just like mounting the guillotine on the
infinitesimal gamble that the axe won't work.
General Hugh Johnson

WITH THE coming of the New Deal came also the New Dealers:
young lawyers, economists, farm experts, finance experts, and
even experts on who was an expert. Mostly they were idealistic,
although they liked to disguise their idealism behind a mask of
practicality and "hard realism." Mostly, too, they were from the
universities, recommended by Felix Frankfurter or Raymond
Moley; brought from the Midwestern schools by Henry Wallace;
friends of friends or, more likely, friends of Justice Louis Brandeis. The staid civil servants in Washington more often than not
viewed the New Deal program with conservative dismay and the
New Dealers themselves with barely disguised repugnance. "We
stood in the city of Washington on March 4th," Raymond
Moley later recalled, "like a handful of marauders in hostile
territory."

But as "Roosevelt's young men" began to flood into the capital, they gave it an entirely new air. Suddenly it was no longer
the somnolent, almost provincial capital it had been for decades

(except in wartime); now it took on a cosmopolitan, energetic aura. Conversation on topics other than golf scores was suddenly fashionable; so was hard work, so were ideas. A disgruntled administrator of the "old school" summed it up wryly: "A plague of young lawyers settled on Washington. They all claimed to be friends of somebody or other and mostly of Felix Frankfurter and Jerome Frank. They floated airily into offices, took desks, asked for papers and found no end of things to be busy about. I never found out why they came, what they did, or why they left." It was certainly true that many of them were former students of Felix Frankfurter from the Harvard Law School; it was also true (as Sherwood Anderson observed after visiting the Department of Agriculture) that they imparted a "curiously exhilarating feeling" to the government offices. Since it was always safer to attack an administrator or an advisor than to attack a politically popular elected official, many of the New Dealers were singled out as symbols for the hate which New Deal policies aroused in conservative quarters. Long before he dared attack Roosevelt, for example, newspaper magnate William Randolph Hearst (who, to his everlasting regret, had actually supported FDR during the election campaign) began to snipe against such men as Felix Frankfurter ("the Iago of this administration!"). But carpings and criticisms rolled off New Deal backs easily in 1933; there was too much to be done and done quickly.

Roosevelt, and many of his advisors, felt that the New Deal program would stand or fall on the success or failure of the new farm policies which were all bound up in the complicated package of the Agricultural Assistance Administration under Secretary of Agriculture Henry A. Wallace and his Assistant Secretary, Rexford Tugwell. Wallace himself seemed perfectly at home in the Department of Agriculture, and for good reason. His father, Henry C. Wallace, had been Secretary of Agriculture under Harding. Famed as a plant geneticist (especially for his development of hybrid corn) and as an editor back in his native Iowa, Henry A. Wallace lived and breathed the age-old grievances of American farmers. He was to be attacked as a radical in later

HENRY A. WALLACE

years, but his was a most conservative radicalism, born and bred in the Bible Belt of the Midwest, concerned not so much with changing the American agricultural system as reforming it, making sure that the American farmer had a secure place within a capitalistically organized farming industry. "When former civilizations have fallen," Wallace said in 1933, "there is strong reason for believing they have fallen because they could not achieve the necessary balance between city and country." It was his purpose to restore that balance. Basically this was to be done by making sure that farmers received higher payment for their products and making sure that the dollars they received in payment would buy as much manufactured goods as the city dollar would buy farm goods.

Something had to be done, and done fast. Although the change of administration in Washington might promise better times down on the farm, the effects of reform could not be felt quickly enough for most farmers. The slide in farm prices, the foreclosures, the thousands of families trekking westward from aban-

doned farms—all this did not cease on March 4, 1933. If anything, it grew worse during the first summer of the New Deal.
The Farmers Holiday Association, under the leadership of one
Milo Reno, had been organized in Iowa in 1932 and quickly
spread throughout the Midwest. Reno urged farmers to "take a
holiday," to withhold their produce from the market until they
could be sure of decent prices. Farmers' strikes had erupted in
Iowa, the Dakotas, Kansas—everywhere through America's agricultural belt. The object was very frankly to starve the cities into
recognizing the farmers' just complaints. And the farmers enforced their strikes: a truck carrying produce to town in a strike
area would inevitably be stopped by gnarled, weather-beaten men
dressed in faded blue jeans, their eyes hard, shotguns and pitchforks at the ready. Violence brought the National Guard, and
bloody clashes took place. Very large areas of Midwestern states
were clamped under martial law by their harried governors. Local
businessmen in market towns and cities, seeing financial ruin in
farmers' strikes, were beginning to organize themselves into self-
styled "vigilante" groups and were hiring gangsters to shoot down
the striking farmers. *The New York World-Telegram* said in the
spring of 1933: "Americans are slow to understand that actual
revolution already exists in the farm belt." This was the essential
problem faced by Wallace and Tugwell, and their weapon, the
Agricultural Assistance Administration, was untried.

Wallace's first task was deeply distasteful to him. It was to
carry out a policy of crop destruction. For, in a capitalist economy, an oversupply of anything would inevitably lead to lower
prices. Industry could control its production according to its estimates of the market, so why not the farmers? If farm prices were
abysmally low, the response had to be a curtailment of farm products to the point where consumers (or, more accurately, food
processors) would pay more for them. Unfortunately, Congress
delayed passage of the AAA beyond the point where crop control
could be arranged by simply withholding land from production.
By the time the AAA had been set up, the spring (1933) crops
had been planted, and the summer fields promised a bumper crop

which could only depress farm prices even further. Destruction was the only remedy left, no matter how distasteful. "To destroy a standing crop goes against the soundest instincts of human nature," said Wallace. And there were many, himself included, who reflected on the bitter irony of destroying crops while many thousands of people were starving. But given the basic organization of the American economy—production for profit rather than for use—there seemed nothing else to do. The fields burned, and thousands and thousands of acres of corn, cotton, wheat, and other staples went up in flames or were ploughed under. For destroying their crops, farmers received benefit payments from the AAA.

More dramatic than the destruction of crops in 1933 was the enforced slaughter of more than six million little pigs. This proposal had come from the farm leaders themselves as a desperate attempt to forestall a glut on the world pork market. Once again it was a question of price: if those millions of pigs grew into hogs and were sold, pork prices would fall to the vanishing point; they were already below the cost of raising the pigs. So the piglets died. And millions of Americans (in the cities, not on the farms) were horrified. When thousands of little pigs overran the stockyards in Chicago and Omaha and ran squealing through the city streets that autumn of 1933, newspapers could not control their indignation at the "massacre of the innocents." "To hear them talk," Wallace ruefully observed, "you would have thought that pigs were raised for pets." Some pork was salvaged out of the slaughter, and about one million pounds were distributed by government agencies to the needy. But nine tenths of the yield had to be thrown away. Once again, it was painfully apparent that something was desperately wrong with a system that destroyed food wholesale while people starved, in America and all over the world. "The people who raise the cry about the last hungry Chinamen are not really criticizing the farmers, or the AAA," Wallace pointed out, "but the profit system."

But destruction as a means to control farm output largely came to an end in 1933; thereafter the government would be able to restrict planting. In October of 1933, Jesse Jones, the Texas banker Roosevelt had appointed to head Hoover's old Reconstruction Finance Corporation, set up the Commodity Credit Corporation which loaned money to farmers who agreed to restrict production. The loans were set at a figure higher than the market price for the crops and therefore acted as a price-support system. If, on the other hand, the market price should rise above what had been loaned, the farmers could pay back the loans and resume production.

By late November, with farm mortgages taken over by government agencies and money trickling into the countryside through RFC, CCC, and other federal organizations, farm violence gradually came to an end. So highly did farm leaders think of AAA restrictive planting policies that many groups—cotton farmers in the South, tobacco planters, potato growers in Maine—sought in the following years to make crop control compulsory by law rather than voluntary. But Wallace stoutly resisted the farmers' own attempts to regiment themselves. He sought cooperation through incentive rather than punishment.

The Secretary of Agriculture found himself beset by other problems, too, problems of conflicting ideas and personalities within his Department. AAA Administrator George Peek, an old battler for farmers' rights, and many of the men Peek brought with him, thought almost entirely in terms of farm income. Their aim was to help farmers; other segments of the economy would have to look out for themselves. Furthermore, they deeply disliked the idea of reducing farm production. Their solution to low prices was to have the federal government subsidize the cost of production on farms and regain what money it could by dumping farm surplus abroad for whatever price it might bring. They did not seem to realize that in a depression-beset world there was no longer a market for American surplus at any price. Opposing the views of Peek and his followers were Rexford Tugwell and AAA General Counsel Jerome Frank (one of Frankfurter's bright young men). Into the AAA, Tugwell and Frank had brought such brilliant young attorneys and economists as Adlai Stevenson from

Chicago, Thurman Arnold and Abe Fortas from Yale, and Alger Hiss, Lee Pressman, John Abt, and Nathan Witt from Harvard. Also a perhaps inevitable enemy of Peek's views was Frederic Howe, who headed the all-but-powerless AAA section which was supposed to look after consumers' interests.

The Tugwell-Frank group were more interested in long-range reform than simply in immediate farm relief. They advocated programs to fundamentally improve the status of tenant farmers, sharecroppers, farm laborers, and migratory workers, and to crack down on the big farm middle-men: the meat packers, the canners, the milk distributors, and the textile millers. As feelings between the Peek group and the reformers grew steadily worse, Roosevelt was forced to intervene. He decided, characteristically, to support the reformers, but to retain the immediate-relief program of the AAA, for the time being at least. Thus Peek was replaced in December, 1933, by Chester Davis, Montana Commissioner of Agriculture, but the program of cutting back production in return for federal subsidies was continued.

During Roosevelt's first term, gross farm income increased by 50 per cent, crop prices increased dramatically, and rural debts were largely reduced. But this was not entirely because of the AAA. For if the New Deal had decreed a cutback in farm production, Nature now began to help the New Deal along. In 1934 the first of the great dust storms that were to lay waste huge areas of the Midwest descended on the nation. The droughts and black blizzards did much more to reduce production and indirectly raise prices than the New Deal could. It was almost as if Nature, offended by man's daring to plough under her abundance, had said, "All right, you want to cut production? I'll show you how to *really* cut production!" But the story of the Dust Bowl and the continuing struggle against rural poverty belongs to a later chapter. The New Deal had come to grips with the farm problem, using the AAA as its chief weapon. And if some of the hardest and harshest agricultural problems remained to be solved, a beginning had been made; the farmers were no longer patroling roads with shotguns. Rexford Tugwell may well have put his finger on the key to AAA success when he said, "Under this plan it will *pay* farmers for the first time, to be social minded, to do something for all instead of for himself alone."

But if farmers, or many farmers at least, could be bribed to act as if they had a social conscience, what about businessmen? The National Recovery Administration (NRA) had been conceived as a twin pillar with the AAA for national industrial recovery. And originally it had contained the means of stimulating businessmen's self-interest in the form of a $3.3-billion public works appropriation. NRA's director, General Hugh Johnson, had understood that this money, by being advanced or withheld from projects within the territory or the competence of various industries, would serve as both carrot and stick to get businessmen to cooperate with the government's program. But even before the NRA had become law, Roosevelt had separated the public works section from the main bill. That $3.3 billion was now being administered by the Public Works Administration (PWA) under the redoubtable Secretary of the Interior, Harold Ickes, and he was interested primarily in the worth and social benefit of projected dams, highways, town halls, and post offices, and in how many men could be speedily employed on these projects, and not at all interested in whether or not any particular industry ought to be either beaten or fed carrots. So General Hugh Johnson started out with a handicap from the very beginning.

Hugh S. Johnson had been born in a small town in the Indian Territory (the Cherokee Strip), had graduated from West Point in the same class as General Douglas MacArthur, had served in the Philippines and had chased Pancho Villa in Mexico with General Pershing, had planned and administered the Draft Act in 1917, and had become the Army's representative on the War Industries Board. Later (in 1919) he resigned from the Army and went into business, being associated variously with George Peek in Chicago and Bernard Baruch in New York, had lost a fortune in the Wall Street Crash, had campaigned for Al Smith in 1928 and Roosevelt in 1932. His career had also included the writing of children's books and the study of law at the University of California. Of all the New Dealers, he was in many ways the most colorful. His voice could boom like a foghorn (and generally did) or wheedle softly; his language was, to say the least, very plain. He had a tendency to treat businessmen as he might have treated Pancho Villa's raiders, and spoke, in his salty Western slang, of "rounding up" industries like so many head of cattle. He was impeccably honest, very hard working, dedicated to the New Deal, and he drank too much, but only occasionally. He gathered together his NRA staff in just four days. As his General Counsel he chose Donald Richberg, veteran of many a reform movement, an able lawyer, and a man well known to labor leaders.

Johnson's immediate task was to negotiate pacts, or code agreements, with America's industries. These codes, which were to be exempt from Sherman Anti-Trust Act prosecution, were to allow various corporations in any industry to set enforceable standards of production, prices, and marketing. They were, as Johnson explained, to "eliminate eye-gouging and knee-groining and ear-chewing in business." They were also to provide minimum standards of fair treatment for labor, especially the elimination of child labor, the setting of minimum wages in each industry, and the fixing of maximum hours. They were to recognize labor's right to bargain collectively. Somewhere along the line consumers' interests were supposed to be protected, too, but this turned out to be a problem beyond solving.

Johnson threw himself into code-making negotiations with all the zest of a frontiersman fighting Indians. But by July he had managed to gain agreement only from the cotton textile manufacturers among the larger industries. Industrial production had doubled since March, but in July a new shock wave hit the stock market and both Roosevelt and Johnson grew alarmed. It seemed that something more effective would have to be thought of to get industrialists to cooperate. The something-more-effective turned out to be a huge nationwide campaign of publicity. Under the symbol of a blue eagle (sketched by Johnson himself) beneath the words "WE DO OUR PART," the NRA undertook to mobilize public opinion to force businessmen to cooperate. The campaign had the earmarks of a holy war conducted like an old-time revivalist meeting. Huge crowds filled auditoriums across the country to hear NRA speakers; parades in which thousands marched were organized in cities and towns; placards bearing the blue eagle appeared in every shop window, on automobile bumpers, on banners, even on children's cribs. The Blue Eagle Parade in New York was the largest in that city's history as a quarter of a million people marched up Fifth Avenue while millions cheered. Eventually more than two million employers signed the NRA pledge.

With public opinion mobilized as if for war, Johnson sped around the country in an Army plane, threatening and cajoling the large corporations of the nation's top ten industries to write and sign codes. By August, 1933, he had gained acceptance from shipbuilding, woolens, textiles, and the electrical industry. He bludgeoned the oil industry into accepting a code, bribed the steel industry into one, soft-talked the lumbermen, and finally won acceptance from the automobile industry (all save Henry Ford, who considered the whole thing a sinister plot). The last to sign were the soft-coal mine operators. But by the end of September, Johnson had the big ten in NRA—on paper, anyhow.

Businessmen in scores and hundreds tramped the corridors of NRA headquarters in the Commerce Building in Washington. They sweated through hard negotiating sessions with labor representatives and NRA administrators, haggled among themselves, and grappled with baffling problems. How, for example, was the barbershop industry to be organized? What rules should strip-tease showmen adopt? (They decided to limit burlesque houses to four strips a day.) Over it all presided General Johnson, basing his whole gamble basically on the patriotism of the businessmen. A man who violated an NRA Code, explained the gruff general would suffer: "As happened to Danny Deever, NRA will have to remove from him his badge of public faith and business honor and 'takin of his buttons an' cut his stripes away,' break the bright sword of his commercial honor in the eyes of his neighbors—and throw the fragments—in scorn—in the dust at his feet . . ."

Unfortunately, the largest corporations proved immune to Kiplingesque threats. They used the codes to establish uniform *high* prices which soon had millions of housewives up in arms. And to satisfy the letter of the code regarding labor, they often created company unions (owned and operated by and for the benefit of the company, not the workers) and plainly demonstrated that any real advances labor was to make would have to be won through prolonged and probably bloody struggle. Old-line Progressives criticized the codes because they created monopolies. New Dealers feared that the high prices set would retard recovery. In March, 1934, Roosevelt was finally forced to appoint a board headed by lawyer Clarence Darrow to review NRA procedures. The Darrow committee reported that NRA practices were permitting big business to squeeze out small business, exploit labor, and gouge the public. The majority of the committee, however, offered no solution but a return to free enterprise (which they described as "wolfish"), while Darrow and one other committeeman advocated socialized ownership of industry.

Roosevelt, although he did not act on the committee's primary recommendations, did begin to halt government agreement to price-fixing and began to support the conservative Donald Richberg's contention that NRA ought to stop bullying businessmen. If this seemed an attempt to ride two horses going in different directions, it was. For not even Roosevelt could bring success to the NRA. It had been, basically, an experiment in business-government *cooperation*. But businessmen would not really cooperate, and General Johnson interpreted cooperation as coercion. In September, 1934, Roosevelt regretfully forced Johnson to resign, replacing him by a board of administrators. Not far off lay the day when the Supreme Court would declare almost all the provisions of the NRA unconstitutional, and since that time many critics have considered the experiment a complete and total failure.

But this criticism seems too harsh. Industry was moving steadily towards concentration, with giant corporations swallowing smaller ones, before, during, and after NRA. Prices rose not only through NRA acquiescence, but also—and primarily—through devaluation of the dollar. Small businesses objected less to the threat of monopolies than they did to NRA's attempt to force fair labor dealings upon them. And NRA did provide jobs for two million workers, stopped the deflationary spiral, improved business ethics, won at least acceptance in principle for minimum wages and maximum hours, and all but wiped out child labor. In a sense, NRA's very success was its own undoing. Although it did little to speed recovery, it at least prevented things from getting worse. And since its only real power lay in public opinion stimulated by crisis, as the crisis eased and public opinion support faded, the NRA increasingly became a general staff without an army. While the AAA found a means to regulate agriculture on a voluntary basis within the framework of a free capitalist economy, NRA could find no permanently effective weapons to achieve the same result in industry. Its only potential weapon of bribery, as has been pointed out, was removed from it at the very beginning when the giant PWA program was transferred to the Secretary of the Interior.

Interior Secretary Harold Ickes, known variously as "the old curmudgeon," "honest Harold," or "that ――― at Interior," depending on the viewpoint, was an old-line Progressive, a follower of Teddy Roosevelt. As such he was dedicated to conservation and reform. He was also old enough to recall vividly the scandals which had beset federal administrations since the turn of the century whenever they attempted to spend government money to improve the public domain. He was determined that PWA funds would not find their way into grafters' pockets, nor become the axle grease of local political machines. Furthermore, he was anxious that whatever projects were undertaken by PWA would be permanently useful, well-constructed, and well-planned additions to the nation's physical heritage. So, while New Dealers like Tugwell and Harry Hopkins viewed PWA spending as a means to stimulate the economy and provide employment and relief, Ickes (with Roosevelt's support) felt no sense of urgency in getting the PWA program under way.

In the end PWA was used to conserve, to beautify, to construct what was permanently needful according to careful blueprints, rather than as a means (except indirectly) of providing relief from depression. By 1939 the program had been, in its social if not its economic aspects, a huge success. PWA helped to rebuild the U.S. Navy; carriers *Yorktown* and *Enterprise* were PWA projects. It modernized and paved thousands of miles of state and federal highways. It helped build the Triboro Bridge in New York City and the Tennessee Valley dams, Boulder Dam, Grand Coulee Dam. It gave Chicago a new sewer system, Denver a water supply system. It built more than fifty airports, the port of Brownsville, Texas, and the overwater highway that connected Key West to Florida. It constructed (between 1933 and 1939) 70 per cent of the nation's new school buildings, 65 per cent of its new courthouses and city halls, 35 per cent of its hospitals and health facilities, and 10 per cent of its subway systems. All this was accomplished without a single proven case of fraud, graft, or corruption. Harold Ickes' passion for honesty and efficiency was a shining example of administrative ability and resulted in a tremendously improved national estate.

But PWA projects were slow to start, and in 1933 millions remained unemployed. Their plight was immediate and urgent. The "hundred days" had produced a Federal Emergency Relief Administration, headed by Roosevelt's former New York State Relief Administrator, Harry Hopkins. Hopkins had thrown himself energetically into the task of distributing FERA funds to state and local relief agencies on a crash basis. But Hopkins continued to view direct relief as damaging to people's morale. Why not, he asked, give the unemployed weekly pay checks in return for socially useful and necessary work? The useful work in this case would not be some giant construction project, blueprints for which would take months to develop, but immediate jobs that had to be done. The object of this class of federal works would be simply to put people to work. During the fall of 1933, with another winter of despair facing the nation, Hopkins convinced Roosevelt of the necessity for an immediate and massive public works program geared to the problems of the unemployed. On November 15, 1933, the Civil Works Administration was formally inaugurated (with Hopkins as its chief), and it proclaimed a goal of giving employment to four million people within thirty days! Although it was to be sixty days before that massive goal was reached, Hopkins and his staff created the largest public employment project in the history of the world with amazing rapidity.

CWA jobs included the repairing and maintenance of roads and highways, the building and repairing of schools and public buildings, the developing of public playgrounds, the hiring of more than 50,000 teachers to open adult education courses in towns and cities. CWA sent thousands more teachers into poverty-stricken rural areas, waged large-scale combat against agricultural insect pests, built over 500 airports. When no other work was immediately available, CWA workers cleared snow, raked leaves, collected trash—anything and everything that had to be done and could be done by people out of work. The very speed with which CWA swung into action (and the fact that its programs were locally administered) condemned the program from the start to a certain amount of corruption and scandal. However, cases of graft were few and inevitably exposed by Hopkins himself. Perhaps more damaging to the CWA's image was the ridicule with which certain businessmen and newspapers viewed some of the emergency projects. The idea that a man should be paid to rake leaves in a public park struck some people as terribly funny, especially people who had never been poor or unemployed. It struck others as government competition in the labor market. After all, with millions of men out of work, industry ought to be able to pay very low wages, but businessmen found they could not pay wages lower than those paid by CWA, to their great irritation.

Whatever its critics might say of it, CWA was a great success with the unemployed. It gave them a chance to work for their money rather than to take handouts. A CWA investigator reported from Sioux City, Iowa: "In Sioux City they actually had fist fights over shovels!" Another CWA administrator reported: "It was pathetic to watch some of the reactions. I saw a few cases leave the office actually weeping for sheer happiness." But happiness among the unemployed was expensive. CWA had spent about $1 billion by February of 1934, and as economic tensions eased its critics became more and more vocal. Conservatives feared that CWA would undermine people's self-reliance. Henry Ford stated that boys riding freight trains aimlessly across the country were getting "the best education in the world." Robert Wood of Sears, Roebuck & Company demanded that relief be given only "on a bare subsistence allowance." Roosevelt himself was worried about the drain on the federal budget represented by CWA activities, and in February, 1934, he finally ordered Hopkins to bring CWA to an end, transferring many of its projects to FERA, others to state and local administrations. The decision was viewed as a triumph of conservatism, but this triumph did not solve the continuing problem of unemployment.

By late fall of 1933, Roosevelt was finally willing to experiment with the value of the dollar—that is, how much gold a dollar could buy—on the theory that lessening the gold content of the dollar would put more of them into circulation, raise commodity prices, and stimulate recovery. Beginning on October 25, 1933, Roosevelt and Henry Morgenthau, Jr. (who had succeeded ailing William Woodin as Secretary of the Treasury) met every morning in the President's bedroom and set the price of gold over breakfast. The price always varied (to make sure that speculators could not guess what it was going to be), and sometimes it seemed to have been arrived at haphazardly. One morning FDR suggested that the price of gold be increased by twenty-one cents. "It's a lucky number," the President said, "because it's three times seven." But the period of fluctuating gold prices (to Morgenthau's great relief) came to an end on January 30, 1934, when Congress, through the Gold Reserve Act, authorized the President to purchase gold from any and all sources at whatever price he deemed suitable. Roosevelt decreed that gold would henceforth be bought at $35 per ounce. This meant that the 1934 dollar was worth (in terms of the amount of gold it would buy) only about 60 per cent of what a 1929 dollar had been worth. But this did not prove to be the great remedy that cheap-dollar advocates had been promising for more than fifty years. It seemed to have but little effect on the national economy. The only tangible result of the Gold Reserve Act of 1934 was the accumulation of gold ingots buried beneath Fort Knox.

The first New Deal brought other ideas, theories, agencies, and men to Washington in 1933 and 1934. There is not room on these pages to describe them all. It was an imaginative, energetic, and large-scale frontal assault on the Depression. But despite the fact that industrial output rose slightly and that the number of unemployed dropped by a few million, the essential fact of widespread depression, unemployment, poverty, and social dislocation remained. The government counterattack of 1933 had put an end to the most desperate aspects of crisis and had brought a sense of hope to the people. Yet by 1934 many millions remained in desperate circumstances. And, as it became apparent that early New Deal measures were not proving to be magic solutions to the nation's problems, desperate people were turning more and more to other social and political solutions—some of them extremely radical, some of them nonsensical, some of them dangerous, but all of them deeply rooted in the continuing anguish of the people themselves.

seven Other Voices, Other Dooms

I want all the neighbors to hear me!
I want God Almighty to hear me!
I'm going to shout till the whole country hears!
Doctor Francis Townsend

I used to try to get things done by saying "please."
That didn't work and now I'm a dynamiter.
I dynamite 'em out of my path.
Senator Huey P. Long

Choose today! It is either Christ
or the Red Fog of Socialism!
Father Charles E. Coughlin

In the midterm elections of 1934 the Democrats won a remarkable victory. Historically, as the party in power, they were supposed to lose Congressional seats during a midterm election. But this time the party in power actually gained seats, in both the Senate and the House of Representatives. There could be no doubt of the popular approval of the New Deal. Kansas editor William Allen White observed of Roosevelt: "He has been all but crowned by the people." And this vote of confidence had some solid basis in improved conditions. The national income in 1934 was half again as high as in 1933; nearly five million of the unemployed had found work. The sense of panic and crisis which gripped the nation during 1932 and 1933 had largely evaporated. But these gains were only relative. In 1934 the national income of $48.6 billion was only little more than half of what it had been in 1929, and in 1933 there were still ten million (about one fifth of the potential labor force) unemployed. Furthermore, there were large groups in the population who not only still suffered from the Depression but for whom the New Deal was not apparently working. The central themes of the early New Deal had been industrial planning to be carried out within the framework of NRA, and agricultural planning to be carried out under the AAA. But by 1935 the NRA was involved in all sorts of problems, and the suspicion that its main provisions would soon be struck down by the Supreme Court was widespread. On the other hand, although it had helped many farmers, the AAA had never really concerned itself with the problems of farm laborers and migratory workers and sharecroppers. These problems predated the Depression but were aggravated by it. Finally, the New Deal, by demonstrating that vigorous action was possible, had invigorated its enemies as well as its friends. Its enemies could, in 1935, be found at both ends of the political spectrum—among extreme leftists and extreme reactionaries. An even more basic division was between thoughtful enemies and demagogues.

Among the demagogues, few were more colorful and none commanded a wider audience than Father Charles E. Coughlin, the "radio priest." Born in Canada in 1892, Father Coughlin took over a Roman Catholic parish in the Detroit suburbs in 1925. When the Ku Klux Klan burned a fiery cross in the young priest's churchyard as the community's welcome, Father Coughlin determined to use the new medium of radio to explain his faith to his new parish. In 1926 he began to broadcast over station WJR in Detroit. He called his program "The Golden Hour of the Little Flower," and his entertainingly rich Irish brogue and fiery style of oratory soon won him a large audience. Within two years radio stations in Chicago and Indiana were carrying his program, and his mail began to include checks and donations. When the Depression came, Father Coughlin began to emphasize politics

FATHER CHARLES E. COUGHLIN

rather than religion in his broadcasts and found a ready audience
among the poor and frightened.

He hated capitalism for its competitive spirit, its exploitation
of the defenseless, its replacement of human relations by profit
relations. And like many untutored social philosophers, he had a
fanatical belief in the magic of money. Gold was the disease,
greenbacks or silver the cure. "Long enough," cried Father
Coughlin, "have we been the pawns and chattels of the modern
pagans who have crucified us upon a cross of gold!" As for the
Depression, "the only two ways out are revaluation of our gold
ounce, or repudiation of our debts. One way is Christianity. The
other way is Bolshevism." As for Bolshevism—which in Father
Coughlin's mind became sometimes confused with Wall Street
bankers, Jews, aliens, or simply people he didn't like—the priest
had no use for it whatsoever. Yet during the early years of the
Depression when it seemed advantageous to express a more liberal
line of thought, Father Coughlin praised many reforms which
were despised by conservatives. But as the Depression crisis

passed, he returned to the old standby of anti-Communism as his lure to the afflicted. And the lure certainly worked. By 1935 he was receiving more than 80,000 letters a week from listeners and he had a nationwide audience for his weekly radio program of ten million. His following was so large that he felt himself able to disregard the admonitions of his church superiors. When Cardinal O'Connell of Boston reprimanded him saying, "You can't begin . . . uttering demagogic stuff to the poor. You can't do it, for the church is for *all*," Father Coughlin simply ignored him.

For several years Father Coughlin supported Franklin Roosevelt and the New Deal. Many New Deal policies seemed to be in line with the priest's hazy economic thoughts, and besides, FDR was so popular that to attack him would be to risk losing millions of listeners (and contributors). The radio priest referred to the New Deal as "Christ's deal," and was flattered by the fact that Roosevelt sent such emissaries as Joseph P. Kennedy to cool off the brimstone from time to time. But by 1934, Father Coughlin was beginning to suspect that the New Deal had lost sufficient popular support to enable him to attack it safely. On November 11 of that year he organized a new movement, the National Union for Social Justice, which was to act independently of either of the two major parties. The Union's program called for revaluing the price of gold, nationalization of basic industries, and a guaranteed annual wage. But the Union's aims were becoming more and more confused in Father Coughlin's mind with a deep, abiding, and extremely ugly anti-semitism. More and more his radio talks included hysterical and insulting references to Jews. He claimed, casually, that Alexander Hamilton's real name was Alexander Levine, attacked Americans who had not "the blood of Christianity flowing in their veins," and told a Senate committee, ". . . One hundred years from today Washington will be Washingtenski."

But aside from those who tuned in Father Coughlin for laughs (and they must have been many), the apocalyptic visions of the radio priest found a solidly receptive audience among the urban lower-middle classes—clerks, small shopkeepers, white collar workers, the descendants of Irish immigrants with high hopes and disappointed lives. All these felt the chilling winds of social change and listened. For by 1934 and 1935, the relief rolls in cities and towns were changing their complexions. Formerly they had contained the names almost entirely of workers. Now, more and more, they included those such as unemployed salesmen, broken small businessmen, and out-of-work office employees. Depression had, after four years, wiped out the savings and resources of many in America's lower-middle classes. They were humiliated at the prospect of government relief and, above all, deeply fearful of being forced into the working class (or non-working class, as it so largely was in 1934). These were the people who had followed the capitalist doctrines of hard work, saving, scrimping in order to "improve" themselves, the people whose ambitions and hopes had caused them to thrill to the American dream of rags to riches. They were not against big business or the rich—they wanted to be like them. And now their dreams were thwarted, their hopes blasted. And they had no feeling of solidarity or history of struggle (such as workers had) to fall back upon. They moved from a dream world of hope into a nightmare world of suspicion and hatred. There were many of them. In other nations, especially Germany, they had found a leader and organized to make their nightmare real. This was the very threat implicit behind the ravings of Father Coughlin.

Much less the demagogue but equally confused was Doctor Francis E. Townsend, a retired physician of Long Beach, California. Born in 1867 in a log cabin in Illinois (which he was later to confuse with Abraham Lincoln's log cabin at Springfield), Doctor Townsend had roamed over much of the West before becoming a doctor in 1903. His practice was centered in the Black Hills of the Dakotas for seventeen years. Then he moved to Long Beach where failing health, lack of clients, and ultimately the Depression brought him to enforced retirement. But he secured a job as an assistant public health officer in 1930, and from that vantage point he saw something of the tragedy of the aged.

Every day the poor flocked into Doctor Townsend's office,

DOCTOR FRANCIS E. TOWNSEND

many of them old. Townsend observed "such distress, pain and horror, such sobbing loyalties under the worst possible circumstances" as were to haunt him thereafter. One morning in the fall of 1933, Doctor Townsend looked out his window and saw in the garbage-littered alley below "three haggard, very old women, stooped with great age, bending over the barrels, clawing into the contents." This hideous spectacle was too much for the good doctor. Those women were about his own age, and the insult to their years offered them by the country they had helped to build moved the doctor to action. In September, 1933, Doctor Townsend sent a letter to the local newspaper outlining a plan whereby every American over the age of sixty would be paid a government pension of $150 (later raised to $200) per month. This pension would be paid on the firm understanding that the money would be spent immediately within the month. Thus not only would old people have an income, but their enforced spending would put untold millions of dollars back into circulation, creating a great new demand for goods and services, new industries, jobs for millions. To finance this program Doctor Townsend proposed a national sales tax on all goods and commodities.

It had never been easy to be old in America, unless one was rich. Traditionally old folks were the responsibility of their families. No state government, and certainly not the federal government, had ever assumed any responsibility for the fate of the nation's aged. Certain industries had offered pensions to discharged workers who passed the company age limit, but these were never more than starvation-level pensions. American society, which placed such a high premium on competition, individualism, and success at any price, had no provision in it for the aged, rich or poor. They were the discarded refuse of an impersonal, clattering, fast-moving industrial machine which devoured their strength and skills in youth and left them to their own devices when youth had fled.

The Depression hit America's old people harder than any other group, with the exception of Negroes. To the vast majority of already poor old folks were now added many, many thousands who had lost their homes, their farms, their insurance policies. Furthermore, like as not, their children or grandchildren were also thrown out of work, and the burden they placed on struggling families became intolerable. They had worked hard and long, saving whatever small amounts they could against the day of retirement. They had often denied themselves much in life so that their declining years might have some touch of independence and dignity. But even this modest hope of reward was wiped out by the Depression. They could look around them at the country built by their sweat and sacrifice and realize they were no longer wanted in it.

It was no wonder, then, that Doctor Townsend's angry letter to the newspaper provoked an immediate response among older citizens. Soon the doctor had organized a movement—Old Age Revolving Pensions, Inc.—and to it flocked the aged by the hundreds of thousands. Townsend clubs, springing up first in California, soon spread all over the country. There old folks came (and some youngsters, too) to be assured that one day they would receive $200 a month and live in security and dignity. Mostly these people had never engaged much in politics. Mostly they had supported such moral crusades as Prohibition in the past. They listened avidly to Townsend's "ministers," sang old-time hymns, and gave their meetings the atmosphere of religious revivals. They sent their pitifully small sums to the OARP, and these sums added up when they were multiplied by a million. Many of them thought of Townsend as Christ reborn; many others considered him the greatest American since George Washington. The measure of their faith was the measure of their distress. When, in January, 1935, Townsend launched the *Townsend National Weekly* magazine, its circulation rapidly reached 200,000.

Orthodox and New Deal economists were for once agreed: the Townsend plan of revolving pensions was impossible. Experts estimated that there would be ten million old people qualified to receive benefits, and this would cost not less than $24 billion a year. That would mean that one twelfth of the American population would receive more than half of the national income. Furthermore, a sales tax would put the burden for paying this huge sum squarely on the shoulders of those least able to afford it—the poor. But so great had the political power of the Townsendites grown that Congress shuddered when a Townsend bill came up for a vote. No Senator or Representative could afford to come out against Mother. Congressman John Tolan of California (where Townsendites accounted for hundreds of thousands of votes) told his colleagues that his mother appeared to him in dreams to admonish gently, "Son, you be good to the old folks, and God will bless you." But despite these angelic whisperings, Congress managed to vote down the Townsend bill, with hundreds of members absent and the rest scrupulously avoiding a roll-call vote.

New Dealers were already brooding over something new—a social security program which would include not only old folks but also the unemployed. But the plan under discussion since 1934 would probably provide much less than $200 per month

HUEY P. LONG

to the aged, and in any event payments under it would not start until 1941. Despite the distant rumblings of the social security plan, Townsendites began to turn their heaviest artillery against Roosevelt and the New Deal. The good doctor began to think of himself as a great political leader, comparable to Lincoln, who, he pointed out, was "just a poor lawyer, no smarter than me . . ." And yet, whatever his personal delusions, Doctor Townsend and his organization reflected not hatred, but kindliness. Townsend would never allow racist or religious bigotry among his followers (many Townsend clubs were desegregated, a notable step in those years), nor would he have any truck with anti-democratic philosophies. He had called the nation's attention to the cruel fate of its old people, and, by and large, he kept faith with the trust they reposed in him. If his plan was unworkable, fantastic, the impulse behind it was decent and humanitarian.

On the other hand, the impulses behind the amazing climb to power of Huey P. Long, Louisiana's famed "Kingfish," and perhaps the man who came closest to being a native American candidate for dictator, were certainly mixed. Like the problems which had given rise to Townsendism, the troubles which were exploited by Huey Long had appeared long before the Depression and were to long survive it. They were rooted in the defeated dream of a slave aristocracy in the South, in the desperate racism of ignorant and viciously exploited people.

The State of Louisiana had known little but misgovernment since the end of the Civil War. With the brief exception of a progressive Negro-White reconstruction government in the late sixties (supported by federal bayonets), the state had long been in the grip of exploitive agricultural and industrial interests. The upstate sugar, cotton, and rice planters had formed an unholy alliance with public utilities corporations and such industrial giants as Standard Oil of Louisiana to exploit every resource, including human resources. No state had a higher level of illiteracy, worse roads, more wretched schools, harsher conditions of labor. In Louisiana little children worked long hours in fields and mills and factories for a few cents a day. The natural rebelliousness of oppressed people had for decades been siphoned off in hatred of Negroes. A carefully calculated, consciously planned campaign to maintain race hatred as a way of life among Louisiana's "poor whites" had long been the policy of political and industrial leaders in the state. This kept the masses of the poor divided and gave them a scapegoat for poor-white frustrations and anguish. No state was a more natural breeding ground for radicalism and violence.

Huey Long was born in 1893 in the town of Winnfield in Winn Parish, Louisiana. Winn Parish had voted against secession in 1860, followed the Populist agrarian movement of the nineties, and had become, uniquely in the South, a stronghold of Socialism during the years before World War I. All that went by the board during the twenties, but Huey Long remembered his father saying, "There wants to be a revolution, I tell you . . . what do these rich folks care for the poor man? They care nothing—not for his pain, his sickness, nor his death." In 1910 Huey Long won a scholarship to Louisiana State University, but lacking the money

to support himself while at school, he became a traveling sales-
man. In 1914 he entered Tulane Law School in New Orleans,
completed a three-year course in just eight months, and became a
lawyer at the age of twenty-one. In 1918 he won the elective office
of Railroad Commissioner by heartily denouncing the big corporations and utilities, and during the next nine years he took
every opportunity to dramatize himself as the champion of the
poor against "the interests." He bid unsuccessfully for the Gov-
ernorship in 1924 (he refused to join the Ku Klux Klan), but in
1928, campaigning under the slogan, "EVERY MAN A KING,
BUT NO ONE WEARS A CROWN," he was elected Gov-
ernor. His campaign tactics had been to pour hell-fire and brimstone down upon the heads of the rich. His raw, blustering,
barely grammatical speeches drew huge and appreciative crowds
of backwoodsmen and poor-white farmers at every crossroads.
Then, to the vast horror of the public utilities and industrial
oligarchs of the state, Huey demonstrated that he really believed
everything he had said. He refused to make the traditional bar-
gains with them, and when he came to the state house at Baton
Rouge he opened a campaign to destroy the political power of
the rich and concentrate it not in the poor but in himself. "I'm
the Constitution around here now," Long declared.

By 1930, Huey Long had effectively destroyed free government
in Louisiana. By a combination of bribery, terrorism (carried out
by his personal corps of state police), and outrageous flouting of
state laws, he had made the state legislature into his own rubber-
stamp gang of yes-men. He passed laws which overrode many
parts of the old constitution and built up a native-American sort
of storm-troop political terrorism. Yet he did not forget the poor.
He gave them new roads, textbooks, a public education system,
hospitals, and a spanking new university at Baton Rouge. He did,
in fact, break the power of the big industrialists and planters, and
if this somehow did not lead to lower prices or higher wages, it
gave satisfaction to the poor whites. Furthermore, although
Huey Long's attitude towards Negroes was what one might
expect from one of his background, he did not stir up racial ten-

sions, and his campaigns were remarkably free from the standard appeals to bigotry and hatred. In 1930 he installed a puppet as Governor and won election to the United States Senate. Louisiana was now his personal domain.

In the Senate Huey quickly won a reputation for vulgarity, disrespect, and clownishness. He treated that august body as if it were a collection of doddering stuffed shirts and, with less justification, absented himself as much as possible from Senatorial business. When Franklin Roosevelt was nominated for the Presidency in 1932, Long supported him vigorously, campaigning for the New Deal throughout the South. But he was fighting for a program he did not fully understand. As New Deal policies unfolded in the months after inauguration, Long found himself more and more at odds with the new administration. Perhaps basically he resented the fact that FDR was so successful a national leader. Roosevelt was, in fact, the embodiment of many of Long's own dreams and aspirations, and he had won his place without resorting to connivance and brutality. The nature of the threat posed by Huey Long was not underestimated in Washington. Everyone was aware that beneath the clowning and semi-literate exterior he maintained, Huey Long had an incredibly fast and comprehensive brain. In 1932, Roosevelt told Rexford Tugwell that Huey Long was one of the two most dangerous men in the country (he named General Douglas MacArthur as the other).

In January, 1934, Long organized the Share-Our-Wealth Society, with chapters in every state. He appointed preacher and old-hand rabble-rouser Gerald L. K. Smith as director of the movement. Share-Our-Wealth proposed that every American family be given a $6,000 "grub-stake," or homestead allowance. Minimum hours would be set for labor, agricultural output would be government controlled, everyone over sixty would receive a federal pension. All this was to be financed by simply confiscating the largest American fortunes through taxes. The fact that even if the government taxed the rich right out of existence it would still not collect anywhere near enough money to give everyone

$6,000 was immaterial to Long and Smith. They wanted a national organization, and now they had one. Gerald L. K. Smith soon proved himself to be a great spellbinder. H. L. Mencken described him as "a boob-bumper worth going miles to see." As Share-Our-Wealth grew in following, Long saw it more and more as a new political party. He said the Democrats and Republicans reminded him of the patent-medicine vendor who sold two bottles: one marked High Popalorum, the other Low Popahirum; the one made by stripping the bark off trees from the top down, the other by stripping bark from the ground up.

By 1935, Huey felt himself a man of destiny. "Fine. I'm Mussolini and Hitler rolled in one. Mussolini gave them castor oil; I'll give them tabasco . . ." But despite this self-description, Huey Long was not a Fascist in the European style. He was more like a South American general who had seized power in some troubled equatorial republic. And it was in the tradition of such a "strong man" that he died. At 9:20 on the evening of September 8, 1935, while the Kingfish swaggered up to the Governor's office in Baton Rouge, surrounded by his menacing bodyguards and state troopers, a young Baton Rouge doctor named Carl Austin Weiss stepped up and shot him with a 32-caliber pistol. The assassin was immediately cut down by gunfire by Long's bodyguards (leaving the nation to speculate why and even if Weiss had actually been the killer), but thirty hours later, on September 10, Huey Long died. He was sincerely mourned by many hundreds of thousands of Louisiana's poor, and his Share-Our-Wealth Society now fell into the hands of Gerald L. K. Smith.

There were others, of course. There was the intelligent and mild Upton Sinclair, world-renowned author, American-style Socialist, utopian, and sincere admirer of Roosevelt and the New Deal. He ran for Governor of California in 1934 under the slogan "END POVERTY IN CALIFORNIA" (EPIC) with a program of taking over idle factories and land and putting both to work by and for the unemployed under cooperative ownership. Sinclair was defeated after a political campaign which may have set some sort of record in American history for "dirty politics." His opponents employed advertising agencies and the skills of Hollywood to produce fake newsreels, alarmist radio broadcasts, etc., thereby introducing into American political life new abuses of the mass media which were to become more familiar to a later generation. Then there was Lawrence Dennis, self-styled Fascist intellectual, who sought European models for his philosophy of force, achieved a brief notoriety during the thirties, and made a modest living appearing on radio programs requiring a literate Fascist to balance "political spectrum" shows.

By no means as important in terms of numbers, but of more interest in terms of the noise they made, were American Communists. The American Communist Party, founded immediately after the Russian Revolution (in 1919), had faithfully followed an unprofitable line dictated by the parent Russian party all through the twenties. One might have expected the 1929 Crash and subsequent Depression to give the Communists their "big chance." But at the beginning of 1931, Communists claimed only 8,000 party members. In 1933 that number had almost doubled and would rise to about 20,000 later—hardly as many people as a Father Coughlin or a Huey Long could assemble in one Madison Square Garden rally. The reasons for Communist failure during the Depression were many. First of all, the Party's "line," or political program, was hardly inspired. It included dreary repetitions of programs which might have been suitable in Russia in 1917 but could hardly be related to the United States in the thirties. It spoke, inevitably, in a bureaucratic language. It was fantastically unrealistic (the Party's solution to the problems facing American Negroes was the establishment of a separate Negro republic in the South), and it was tied hand and foot to the immediate needs of Russian foreign policy.

Yet the Communists exerted a powerful attraction upon America's intellectual and artistic movement during the thirties. In 1932, the Party's Presidential campaign had attracted the support of such novelists as Theodore Dreiser, Sherwood Anderson, John Dos Passos, Erskine Caldwell; critics such as Edmund Wilson, Lionel Trilling, Clifton Fadiman, and Malcolm Cowley;

and many university professors, headed by Sidney Hook and Henry Dana. It also counted on the secret membership of certain of the bright young lawyers in Roosevelt's entourage; both Alger Hiss and Lee Pressman of the Department of Agriculture were, according to later testimony, members. And intellectual support often came indirectly in the form of eager (almost wishful) acceptance of Marxist thought, if not the Communist Party's immediate political objectives. Why?

There may have been as many reasons as there were intellectual followers. For one thing, the Marxist analysis of capitalism, with its emphasis on capitalism's "internal contradictions" and its predictions of economic disaster in regular cycles, seemed well borne out by the Great Depression. More than that, the entire Marxist view of history seemed to offer a clear and comprehensive understanding of apparently confused and contradictory events. It offered a "system" of thought as complete—and hence satisfying to troubled minds—as a religious faith. Furthermore, Marxist thought and the Communist Party certainly appeared to be on the side of the angels, fighting for the cause of the workers and farmers and Negroes, the exploited and the oppressed. And in the early thirties, not very much was generally known about conditions in Soviet Russia. Travelers came back and reported largely what they hoped (or were permitted) to see. There was no unemployment in the Soviet Union, they said. Subsistence was guaranteed there, and mighty strides towards industrialization were visible on every hand. Apparently invisible, at least at first, were the millions of starving peasants who died in Stalin-sponsored famines and the prisons of the Secret Police.

Communist Party Chief Earl Browder, faithful to the line established at various international Party congresses in Moscow, stuck to a program of all-out attack against Roosevelt and the New Deal during the early thirties. In 1934 Browder characterized the New Deal: "In political essence and direction it is the same as Hitler's program." The Communist Party newspaper, *The Daily Worker*, declared that "Roosevelt, himself a rich cotton planter . . . , personally is interested in making money out of the destruction of cotton." As late as 1935 the Party assured its faithful: "The New Deal is striving toward fascism and war in order to hold the workers in industrial slavery." This nonsense, combined with Communist strong-arm methods at the rallies of such rival organizations as the Socialist Party, soon led to the abandonment of the party line by America's foremost writers and intellectuals. Of those listed as supporting the Party's Presidential ticket in 1932, not one remained a supporter in 1934.

In 1936, with the rise of Hitler's Germany posing new and ominous threats to Soviet Russia, Communist parties throughout the world were ordered by Moscow to adopt new tactics. No longer were they to criticize liberal and progressive groups. Instead they were to attempt to join with them in a "popular front," which would put pressure on national governments to support an anti-Fascist coalition internationally. The American Communist Party obediently reversed itself, and soon the political landscape was dotted with committees, congresses, and organizations devoted to the fight against Fascism, in which the Communist Party line was subdued or muffled.

But it hardly required Communist "plotting" (always inefficient at best) to unite American intellectuals against the Fascist threat. They joined various anti-Fascist groups because of sympathy for the victims of European Fascism and a natural loathing of Naziism, racism, and murder. When the Fascists in Spain, grouped behind General Francisco Franco, opened full-scale civil war against the Spanish Republican Government, American sympathies generally lay with the Republicans. Americans who enlisted in the Lincoln and Washington Battalions of the International Brigade to fight the Franco forces in Spain were, it is true, submitting to Communist leadership and organization, but they were by no means all Communists. They, and the many hundreds of thousands who supported them in the United States, were simply waging a battle for freedom which many understood would one day have to be faced by the entire nation.

The fact that the Lincoln and Washington Battalions were Communist organized and led was mainly because Communists were dedicated activists. They were the ones who were willing to take the initiative and the risks, to stick their own necks out. When John L. Lewis started his great drive to organize the Congress of Industrial Organizations (CIO), he had often to depend on Communist labor organizers and leaders simply because they were the most fearless and efficient. Likewise, many American intellectuals, congenitally disposed to endless argument, endless agonizing over their social consciences, and endless talk, secretly admired the men who, inspired by an all but religious fervor, could subdue their personal qualms and *act*.

In view of the fact that Roosevelt and the New Deal were under almost constant and even vicious attack from the Communists, the later attempt to paint the New Deal as "Communistically inspired" was singularly ridiculous. New Dealers were, to a man, involved in desperate exertions to save the capitalistic system. And in this respect, Communist criticism of the New Deal was correct. Hopkins, Tugwell, Moley, Wallace, and the rest placed their faith in experimentation in an attempt to ameliorate capitalist abuses. Revolutionary solutions which involved subverting or changing the American economic system were repugnant to them politically and personally. The sarcastic response of New Dealers to Communist and conservative attack was perhaps best summed up by Adolf Berle, who observed: "It is just possible that all of the social inventiveness of the world was not exploded between the two poles of Adam Smith and Karl Marx."

But the poles of reaction and revolution generated much lightning during the Great Depression. The fact that this was heat lightning and not celestial thunderbolts was not always apparent at the time. Even canny politician Jim Farley feared that Huey Long's Share-Our-Wealth program might attract as many as six million votes in 1936, a fear which subsequently proved wildly exaggerated. Many of the extremist leaders and their programs seem fantastic today. But millions of Americans took them quite seriously at the time. In truth, the American people had suffered some notable psychological shocks in those days. First there had been the severe shock of the Depression itself; then the shock of the New Deal attempt to combat it. More than that, it seemed that all the old values of American life were being brought into question. The traditional beliefs of Americans had not, it seemed, been of any help in preventing the Depression, and were proving of little help in ending it. Perhaps new ideas, no matter how radical, were required. And, too, the support for radical programs came primarily from those groups which the New Deal program had not helped. The followers of Townsend and Coughlin and Long and Smith were not by any means necessarily vicious. For the most part they were politically naïve, economically depressed, psychologically disturbed, and, above all, frightened by and unable to cope with problems which baffled far keener minds. The rise of extremist movements during the thirties was, in a sense, the social price America had to pay for the collapse of an unbalanced economy and an unfair social order. It was a small price to pay compared to that exacted of such nations as Germany, Spain, and Italy during those years. And, in a more profound sense, American extremism, then as now, was a continuing price to be paid for generations of political undereducation. When the frontier closed, the patent medicine salesmen, with their nostrums and cureells, did not vanish—they simply changed their product.

eight The Second Wave

If liberal government continues over another ten years
we ought to be contemporary
somewhere in the late Nineteen Forties.
Anne O'Hare McCormick

Government by hullabaloo may have been succeeded
in part by government by abracadabra.
Reed Powell

Legislation in the United States is a
digestive process by Congress with frequent
regurgitations by the Supreme Court.
Sir Wilmot Lewis

THE SUMMER and fall of 1934 had seen what some historians have
regarded as a "retreat" on the part of Roosevelt and his New
Dealers. While demagogues stumped the land, there was a strange
and numbing silence in Washington. No large new measures
were proposed, and it seemed that the New Deal was paralyzed by
the knowledge that its first wave of attack against the Depression
had so largely failed to restore prosperity. But plans were being
made during these months, and the humid summer air of the
Capitol was made heavier by endless argument. By and large it
was evident that the hasty measures for relief—AAA, NRA, and
the works program of PWA—had been insufficient in terms both
of relief and of reform which might bring relief. Federal aid to
the unemployed continued under Hopkins' FERA, but CWA

had been brought to an end. Roosevelt finally inclined to those of his advisors who urged that while relief efforts must continue, more emphasis should be placed on basic reform. FDR evidently felt that if early New Deal weapons had failed, new ones must be tried.

In January, 1935, at Hopkins' urging, Roosevelt proposed a gigantic new program of emergency employment. The new measure would give three and a half million jobs, paid at a little less than prevailing wage rates (so that the unemployed would not be discouraged from seeking private employment). The remaining one and a half million people on relief would be turned back to local and state charity organizations as "unemployables." The program would cost nearly $5 billion, making it far and away the largest single appropriation of money by the United States or any other nation in history. Since the entire object of the program was to put people to work quickly, Roosevelt elected to turn the job over to the experienced and energetic Harry Hopkins, rather than to the "monument-minded" Harold Ickes. Hopkins soon had the new agency, the WPA (Works Progress Administration) under way. He was not permitted to compete with private industry, nor with other government (PWA) work projects, and given the magnitude of his task it was perhaps inevitable that many WPA projects took on a "make-work" aspect. But by the time WPA came to an end (in 1940) it had built or improved 2,500 hospitals, 5,900 schools, 1,000 airports, and nearly 13,000 playgrounds. It had done everything from conducting art classes for the insane (in Cincinnati) to running a mobile library (using packmules) in the Kentucky hills.

WPA also pioneered in providing government aid in areas usually neglected. The Federal Theater Project, employing actors, directors, writers, and musicians, not only provided work but it also produced some of the most original and vital theater America had ever seen. And it brought theater to hundreds of thousands of Americans who had never before seen legitimate stage productions. Sinclair Lewis' drama of Fascism's possible take-over in America, *It Can't Happen Here*, opened in twenty-one theaters in eighteen cities simultaneously. Puppet shows for children in city parks, dance theater productions (New York's Henry Street Theater had to call out police reserves to handle overflow crowds at these productions), plays in Yiddish, Spanish, and French, poetry drama (W. H. Auden's *Dance of Death*, T. S. Eliot's *Murder in the Cathedral*)—all these and many, many more were produced by WPA.

In another startling departure from tradition, WPA established a Federal Writers' Project, putting hundreds of writers to work turning out ambitious state guides, ethnic studies, a "Life in America" series, and fiction. The books were published by commercial publishers and included such notable works as *U.S. One, Maine to Florida*; *The Oregon Trail*; *These Are Our Lives*; and the imaginative picture book *Who's Who in the Zoo*. When, in 1939, Congress, in a wave of cutbacks, brought the Federal Theater Project to an end, it permitted the Federal Writers' Project to continue only if local agencies agreed to put up 25 per cent of the necessary money. To Congressional amazement, every one of the forty-eight states immediately came up with the cash.

A Federal Art Project gave employment to hundreds of painters and artists. Some of these taught everything from Indian rope-weaving to fine arts. Others were employed decorating federal buildings, especially post offices. The Art Project splashed millions of gallons of paint on federal walls in the form of murals. Inevitably, many of them were second rate, mostly on the "heroic" scale, showing heavy-muscled workers moving mountains or grim-faced pioneers opening the West. Yet, FDR himself, commenting on Federal Art, found "some of it good, some of it not so good, but all of it native, human, eager and alive."

WPA's National Youth Administration, organized under the leadership of Aubrey Williams, an Alabama social worker, gave part-time jobs to 600,000 college students and one and a half million high-school students. NYA also found work for more than two and a half million youngsters who were not in school. The NYA program was as comprehensive as that of its WPA parent body; it built tuberculosis sanitariums in Arizona, an observatory in Nebraska, a milking barn in Texas, tennis courts in Topeka, and renovated school houses across the nation. Although conservatives brought forward their old hue and cry about "government domination of the schools," by the time NYA came to an end (1941), no instance of federal interference in the schools had taken place.

Although WPA was another, if larger, weapon in the fight against immediate problems of unemployment—intended to provide relief rather than to reform society—it was, like PWA and CWA before it, a stop-gap measure. But even as it swung into action, the New Dealers were preparing a much more vital, permanent, and thorough-going reform. As early as June, 1934, Roosevelt had appointed a special Cabinet committee, headed by Labor's Frances Perkins, to study the problem of social security. On January 17, 1935, FDR asked Congress to enact the Social Security Law. The bill provided a national system of old-age insurance in which most employees would be compelled to participate. When they reached the age of sixty-five, employees would receive retirement annuities financed by taxes both on their own wages and on their employers' payrolls. Their old-age benefits would depend on what they earned during their working life. The plan also provided for a system of federal-state unemployment insurance, and set up a program of federal-state aid to dependent mothers and children, the crippled, the blind, and those over sixty-five who would not be eligible for social security benefits.

Conservatives were outraged by the proposal. It would, they claimed, undermine those great American virtues of self-reliance which permitted people to take satisfaction from providing their own security (and to starve if they couldn't). New Jersey Senator A. Harry Moore declared: "It would take all the romance out of life." Southerners worried that it would undermine the system which kept millions of Negroes in a state of semi-slavery in the cotton, rice, and sugar fields. Townsendites, of course, attacked the measure as not going far enough; social security benefits would be far below their proposed $200-per-month per oldster.

The Social Security Act was, indeed, a conservative law. European nations had long enjoyed social security laws, and in no other nation was social security financed by taxes on workers' wages. Most social security programs were financed entirely by governments as part of their responsibility to their citizens. But in the United States, social security was to be modeled on various private insurance company plans. Roosevelt well understood the implications of forcing the worker to finance his own security (rather than providing it directly out of the profits workers helped to create for giant industries), but he was concerned lest future Congresses attempt to dismantle the law. "We put those payroll contributions there so as to give the contributors a legal, moral and political right to collect their pensions and their unemployment benefits," FDR declared. "With those taxes in there, no damn politician can ever scrap my social security program." And, too, the new law denied social security coverage to many classes of people, notably farm laborers and domestic employees. And by relying on federal-state cooperation in unemployment insurance it nullified that part of the program in most states. Yet, despite these faults, the Social Security Act of 1935 was a landmark in American history. It clearly established government's social responsibility to its citizens and it provided a sound foundation on which future generations could build.

Then, on May 27, 1935 ("Black Monday"), what many New Dealers had long feared came to pass. The United States Supreme Court, in a unanimous 9-to-0 decision, dropped the axe on NRA. It found that NRA had delegated powers to local groups (through the industrial codes) which it had no right to delegate, and it found, too, that the definition of interstate commerce under which the NRA acted (that clause in the U.S. Constitution which provided that the federal government could regulate commerce between the various states) was too broad. By thus attacking NRA on the basis of its assumed powers of regulation, the Supreme Court not only destroyed the entire industrial recovery program but it also threatened eventually to destroy many other New Deal measures. Basically, the Supreme Court was saying that despite the emergency of depression, the federal government was assuming too much responsibility for the individual lives of Americans and interfering too much in a private-enterprise system.

Much of the nation was stunned. If the federal government had no power to relieve distress and reform an economic system which had brought the nation to the edge of disaster, then who had such power? And despite the fact that New Dealers had long worried about the constitutionality of their hastily drawn emergency laws, Roosevelt himself was dumbfounded, not so much by the decision as by its unanimity. Liberal justices such as Louis Brandeis and Benjamin Cardozo had joined their more conservative colleagues in thus attacking the New Deal. FDR declared that the implications of the Supreme Court decision were more important than any since the infamous Dred Scott decision which had, in the years before the Civil War, declared that Negroes could not be considered citizens of the United States. The Supreme Court had leaned heavily on a strict interpretation of the Constitution's commerce clause. FDR insisted that the nation had been "relegated to the horse-and-buggy definition of interstate commerce."

Although opposition to the New Deal on the part of conservative Supreme Court justices was a foregone conclusion (and they held a majority in the 1935 Court), the opposition of liberal justices was unexpected. But such men as Brandeis and Cardozo had their own reasons for being against NRA. They deeply distrusted the idea that industries should be freed from the provisions of the Sherman Anti-Trust Act in order to set up codes of behavior and fix industry-wide wages and prices. This smacked of government support for giant trusts. Brandeis especially had no faith in government regulation of giant industry. He pointed out that government regulatory bodies would inevitably come under the influence and control of the very industrial combines they were meant to regulate. He believed that only by breaking up huge business combinations and enforcing a system of smaller competitive enterprises could economic democracy be assured. His was by no means a reactionary or even a conservative position,

LOUIS BRANDEIS

and the problem to which he addressed himself was not easily solved. Technical advances in industry had made combination inevitable. A large corporation could produce more efficiently than a small one in very many areas. For example, Ford or General Motors, by coordinating and controlling the activities which might have been split up by dozens of companies, could presumably manufacture automobiles faster, better, and more cheaply. Furthermore, the important technical developments in machinery had had the effect of complicating the manufacturing process in the sense that the more complex the equipment, the more expensive it was to install and run—hence only the larger corporations could finance technical progress. But with their growing monopoly on technical progress, large corporations were also developing monopoly of potential markets, and small companies were squeezed out. And not only in such heavy industries as automobiles and steel did large corporations benefit; the fate of the local corner grocery store bore eloquent testimony to the benefits that large-scale buying, processing, and distribution could bring to such giant corporations as the A & P food stores. The questions raised by Brandeis and his associates in 1935 were not easily dismissed; they have still not been solved.

But while Roosevelt felt himself under attack by the Supreme Court—which followed up its NRA ruling by decisions which all but put Wallace's AAA out of business and attacked the idea that the federal government had the right to regulate wages and hours of labor in interstate commerce—he did not respond immediately to the Court's decisions. That would come later. In the meantime, emergency measures were clearly required to replace some of the legislation which the Court had struck down.

It was apparently the impact of the revived conservative opposition to the New Deal which attracted Roosevelt to Brandeis' belief in cutting big business down to size. To FDR this was not so much a change in philosophy (he avoided any kind of broad ideological commitments) as it was a change in direction, weapons, tactics. The Depression had not been banished by his early efforts, and now his program was being assailed by the rich. Very well. After sending the Social Security bill to Congress, the President forwarded recommendations that Senator Robert Wagner's Labor Relations Act be passed; that a Banking Act which would give the federal government more stringent control over banks be adopted; that a Holding Companies Law which would all but destroy that old device for trust establishment be enacted; and, finally, that Congress pass a "Soak-the-Rich" tax bill.

The Wagner Act, which FDR originally opposed, was designed both to preserve the labor provisions of the now defunct NRA and to carry labor's fight for recognition a few steps further. It provided for the establishment of a National Labor Relations Board with power to conduct elections to determine whether employees wanted to be represented by a union. It also restricted employers from such unfair practices as discharging workers for union membership, setting up company unions, and refusing to negotiate with union representatives in good faith. Enacted into law on July 5, 1935, the Wagner Labor Relations Act became labor's charter of independence, its bill of rights. Now, for the first time in history, all the power of the federal government was placed on labor's side of the scales. To what uses this new-found freedom was employed by labor unions belongs to a later chapter. While many viewed the new law as all but revolutionary in its significance, others saw it as simply redressing the economic balance between big corporations and their workers.

Roosevelt's "Soak-the-Rich" tax bill was just what its critics feared—a measure designed to redistribute wealth. It was the first bill ever proposed to Congress which would really reach into the pockets of the wealthy. It proposed a greatly increased tax on inheritances, a heavy tax on gifts, steeply graded taxes on large personal incomes, and a corporate profits tax scaled according to the size of the corporation. Conservative reaction was violent. The new tax proposals raised an outcry on the part of the rich and of the press such as no previous New Deal measure had aroused. Congress debated the bill all summer, struck out the inheritance tax, and reduced the graduated corporate profits tax to nothing but symbolic importance before it finally passed the Wealth Tax Act of 1935. And despite the bitterness engendered by the bill's provisions among the rich, it did not, in fact, bring about any redistribution of wealth. In fact the percentage of the national income received by the wealthiest one per cent of the population actually increased slightly after 1935.

The Public Utilities Holding Company Bill of 1935 was a direct assault on bigness in business. Holding companies, which were corporations which "held" controlling shares of stock in other companies (sometimes to the point where many of them were ten times removed from the original company that actually produced something for consumption), were a business method of escaping the provisions of the Sherman Anti-Trust Law. Especially powerful in the public utilities field, they permitted concentration of ownership behind the mask of independent enterprise. For example, more than one hundred Southern power and light companies, each supposedly independent, were actually controlled through pyramided holding companies in one giant trust. Thus electric power prices were "fixed" over wide areas of the country at an abnormally high profit rate, and the individual companies supplying power could not be prosecuted since they themselves had committed no delinquency under the trust laws. Will Rogers explained succinctly: "A Holding Company is a thing where you hand an accomplice the goods while the policeman searches you." Furthermore, holding companies "milked" the value of the operational companies they controlled mercilessly, inflated the value of their stock, and, by siphoning off profits which might have gone into expansion, prevented the growth of operating company services. It was through a dizzy pyramid of holding companies that Samuel Insull had built his ill-fated empire before the crash of 1929.

Public utilities companies combined to fight this threatening new legislation through the National Electric Light Association. Spending millions of dollars, they flooded the country with pamphlets, hand-outs to newspapers, speakers, and propaganda of every sort. NELA lobbyists put tremendous pressure on Congressmen (the local public utilities corporation back home was generally the heaviest contributor to a Congressman's campaign fund); NELA representatives censored school textbooks to eliminate any disparaging remarks about private power companies; editors, professors, lecturers, and even students were secretly placed on the NELA payroll; letter-writing campaigns were organized to deluge Congressmen with pro-utilities mail from back home. NELA undertook one of the largest propaganda campaigns in American history to fight the Utilities Holding Company Act, and every penny of the cost of this huge campaign was borne by the individual who paid his electric light bill every month.

But, in the end, Congress adopted the new law. All holding companies more than twice removed from operating companies were wiped out. The Securities Exchange Commission (with which all holding companies now had to register) was empowered to eliminate holding companies more than once removed from operating companies if these were found not to be in the public interest, and to supervise the financial transactions of holding companies generally. Within three years almost all of the great public utilities empires would be destroyed.

When Congress finally adjourned in August, 1935, many commentators compared its record to a new "hundred-days" assault on America's economic and social problems. And, since this time the assault had been directed primarily at the pocketbook of business where it hurt most, Roosevelt agreed with those of his advisors who recommended that a "cooling-off" period be allowed. Business confidence had been badly shaken; businessmen should be allowed a breathing space in which to learn that they could indeed live with the new laws, while the country generally should be given time to digest the new legislation. Despite recurring speeches in which he assailed the "economic royalists," Roosevelt was content to relax the New Deal reformist zeal during 1936. Besides, 1936 was an election year (and almost to the end of his days FDR would hope that businessmen would finally see that he was actually saving them from far more radical solutions) in which the Democrats still hoped for some business support.

To oppose Roosevelt, the Republicans nominated Governor Alfred Landon of Kansas and as his running mate chose Chicago publisher Frank Knox. The Landon-Knox team was far more liberal than many Republicans at first suspected. Landon himself approved of most New Deal measures, was personally an admirer of Roosevelt, had fought the Ku Klux Klan in Kansas, and had an excellent record on civil rights. After he won the nomination, Landon did his best to rid his campaign team of the more recalcitrant Republican conservatives (he avoided Hoover's proffered support like the plague). But as the campaign progressed and Landon found himself less and less able to offer more than a "me-too" attitude towards New Deal measures, the Old Guard Republicans became more and more vocal. Liberal Republicans, on the other hand, were distressed by Landon's ineffective public speaking, his awkwardness, his apparent provincialism. Perhaps inevitably, Alf Landon, a good man and one of progressive sympathies, found his campaign attracting primarily outraged conservatives who were almost as much his enemies as they were Roosevelt's.

In truth, many of the nation's rich had developed an all but pathological hatred of Franklin D. Roosevelt and his New Deal. They referred to him as "that man," or "that cripple in the White House," and regaled each other with scabrous jokes about Eleanor Roosevelt and other New Dealers. Salesmen seeking an appointment at corporation offices often handed the receptionist a card reading: "Buy something from me or I'll vote for *him* again!" Many of the nation's wealthiest men contributed large sums of money to such organizations as the Liberty League (formed in 1935) which made up for its lack of any popular appeal by the virulence of its attacks on the New Deal. The DuPont family, for example, attempted to finance a national campaign by Governor Eugene Talmadge of Georgia, whose social, political, and racial views were so definitely Fascistic as to win him the enthusiastic backing of Gerald L. K. Smith. But such activities on the part of the rich reflected, for the most part, political stupidity rather than Fascist conviction. They were important only as an illustration of the fact that in 1936, an American Hitler might have expected to receive that measure of financial support from the deluded men of wealth in America that the real Hitler had received in Germany. This was a measure of the intense rage that FDR had aroused among some (but not all) of the rich. It was based not only on antipathy to New Deal policies, but also, and perhaps most importantly, on the fact that businessmen had now been displaced from the seats of power in America, and they felt a very personal sense of impotence in their dethroning. Nothing in their background had equipped them to understand the social and political upheaval occurring about them. Theirs was a fear of the unknown—the most damaging kind of fear.

In June, 1936, the messiahs of doom joined forces. Huey Long was dead, but his loud-mouthed apostle, Gerald L. K. Smith, brought the remnants of Share-Our-Wealth with him when he joined forces with Father Coughlin and Doctor Townsend. The good doctor felt distinctly uneasy in the company of rabble-rousers such as Smith and Coughlin, but he joined them in forming a third party which nominated Congressmen William Lemke of North Dakota for President. Father Coughlin denounced FDR as "Franklin Double-Crossing Roosevelt," and Gerald L. K. Smith outdid himself in frenzied oratory. H. L. Mencken described one Smith speech as "a magnificent amalgam of each and every American species of rabble-rousing, with embellishments borrowed from the Algonquin Indians and the Cossacks of the Don." Smith proposed that 100,000 storm troopers be enlisted from among the Townsendite youth to "guard" the polls on election day.

The recipient of all this enmity from all these sources, one Franklin Delano Roosevelt, campaigned like a man who enjoyed campaigning. He traveled all over the country, greeting immense and enthusiastic throngs in every city. Mainly he campaigned, not against Landon, but against Herbert Hoover and the "economic royalists." The forces of "organized money," he told one cheering audience, "are unanimous in their hate for me—I welcome their hatred." There was a note of easy confidence in Roosevelt's speeches during the 1936 campaign. And this was based not only on the weakness of his opponents but also on the knowledge that he had forged a new Democratic alliance which was unbeatable. It comprised organized labor (John L. Lewis donated $740,000 to the Democratic 1936 campaign fund), the big-city machines in the North, the big-city Negro vote, and liberals everywhere. To this might still be added, in 1936, the vote of the "Solid South." Predictions of a Roosevelt victory were widespread (except in the columns of the unfortunate *Literary Digest* magazine, which predicted a Landon landslide), but no one was prepared for the magnitude of Roosevelt's victory in November. The Democrats carried every state except Maine and Vermont in the greatest electoral victory since the days of President Monroe. It appeared that not only the Negroes, the big-city machines, the ranks of organized labor, and the Solid South wanted Roosevelt. So, too, did normally staunch Republican farmers in the Midwest, a surprising number of businessmen (both "big" and "little"), and many Republicans who simply could not stomach a return to Hooverism. Alf Landon bore his defeat with his customary good grace and remained a Roosevelt supporter. The Union Party of Smith, Coughlin, and Townsend, already split over objectives and policy, polled a meager 882,000 votes. Townsendism was at an end, Father Coughlin retired from politics, and Gerald L. K. Smith started brooding about how to form an American Nazi Party with German assistance.

The President carried with him so many Democratic Congressmen that it was found impossible to seat all seventy-five Democratic Senators on the Democratic side of the aisle in the Senate; twelve had to sit with the Republicans. The Republican Party seemed doomed. Someone hung a large banner across the highway leading from New Hampshire into Maine which read "You Are Now Leaving the United States." The *New York Times* observed that so great was FDR's influence that "If he were to say a kind word about the man-eating shark, people would look thoughtful and say perhaps there *are* two sides to the question."

There was no doubt that the New Deal was overwhelmingly popular with the American people. But this was not simply because of the Roosevelt charm, nor was it simply because of the success of New Deal measures. Many were unsuccessful; the Depression had not been licked. But the people felt that there was someone in the White House who was, basically, on *their* side. And in 1936, at least, that was sufficient.

nine Grapes of Wrath, Wine of Hope

> The decay spreads over the State, and the sweet smell is a great sorrow on the land . . . and in the eyes of the hungry there is a growing wrath. In the souls of the people the grapes of wrath are filling and growing heavy, growing heavy for the vintage.
>
> *John Steinbeck*

> The government expert was trying to explain. "Now you farmers are just nervous. There's no use looking so far ahead. A step at a time. We're getting relief in here as fast as we can."
>
> "You're not paying us relief," said a farmer. "You're paying the banks relief."
>
> *Josephine Herbst*

FOR MORE years than anyone could remember—for centuries before there was anyone to remember—the great sea of grass had blanketed the plains. The grass was six feet high and tough-rooted, and it spread from Canada down to Texas. The grass was tougher than the weather, its only enemies being the huge herds of buffalo that roamed through it and an occasional prairie fire started by lightning or perhaps the ashes of an Indian campfire. Until the white men came. The pioneers looked out over the boundless, waving horizon and saw things the Indians had never seen. They saw the richest farming land in the world; they saw the boundaries of twenty states or more; they saw hundreds of thousands of homesteads; they saw their own and a nation's future. From about 1858 on they poured into the great grasslands. The herds of buffalo were slaughtered, the Indians dispersed or massacred, and the grass itself attacked. When the grass resisted their ploughs they invented a new kind of steel-shod plough made especially for breaking the soil of the plains. And they cut down the trees to make cabins, houses, and barns. They were right about the land—it was the richest in the world. During the years of World War I it produced millions and millions of bushels of wheat and corn and fed not only America but many nations overseas. When bad times started for farmers in 1921, it was a man-made economic problem, not any fault of the rich Midwestern soil.

But all unknown to the pioneers (such things might be discussed in Eastern universities from time to time, but they were unknown to the farmers on the plains) they had, for seventy-five years, been preparing the land for a disaster. Rainfall was never very great over the sea of grass. But what moisture did descend was trapped by the tough roots of the grass itself and by the roots of the trees so that the soil was nourished and held in place. When the grass and the trees were gone, the moisture ran off into creeks and streams and rivers, carrying the land with it. Then, in 1930, years of drought commenced. Summer sun baked the land; sudden cloudbursts did not penetrate it, and the water level of lakes dropped by five feet or more. And then the wind swept over the land. It picked up the parched, dry soil that had nothing to hold it down and blackened the sky with dust.

In 1931 and 1932 the dust storms were relatively small in western Kansas and eastern Colorado. In 1933 they were worse. In 1934 they were murderous. Great black clouds of dust arose that blotted out the sun, first in the Texas panhandle, but spreading then to the Dakotas and as far east as the Alleghenies. The clouds of dust billowed in the sky—the topsoil of a nation blowing away. The dust drifted like snow or sand—huge banks of it against houses and schools and fences. Business stopped and towns had to turn on their street lights at midday. And the dust—a fine, acrid, yellowish powder—sifted into farmhouses in spite of the wet sheets and rags farm wives stuffed beneath doors and around windows. Even in the big Eastern cities these astonishing clouds of dust turned the sky yellow and red at sunset and brought city dwellers a taste of Midwestern dirt.

The dust buried the crops over millions and millions of acres. And it choked streams and wells and drove cattle and sheep and other farm animals mad with thirst before they died and were buried beneath the dust. In Kansas and Nebraska, the Dakotas and Oklahoma, men spoke of the wrath of God, of divine judgment. And even after the dust subsided in the winter, there was nothing to be done. The land had literally been blown away. What was left was little better than desert; crops would not grow there for many years, perhaps never. Coming on top of the Depression, the great dust storms of 1934 and 1935 completed the ruin of hundreds of thousands of farmers. They might hold out for a while, eating what vegetables they could grow in the backyard, staving off the sheriff one way or another, but in the end they would have to leave. The land no longer wanted them. The farms and homesteads their grandfathers had carved out of a wilderness had returned to wilderness. So it was loading up the family and a few belongings into an old jalopy; it was heading west again—El Dorado had always been to the west. They went not as pioneers now but as desperate migrant workers, seeking refuge anywhere, willing to work for any wages at all, doing the only thing they knew how to do—planting and harvesting other men's lands.

By the thousands they fled the new desert of the Midwest for Oregon and Washington and California. By 1940, one million of them would have migrated towards the Pacific. But it was not El Dorado that awaited them. Towns through which their jalopies rolled hurriedly hung out signs saying "NO BUMS ALLOWED, KEEP MOVING." For these towns were having difficulty enough finding tax and charity money for their own poor. The migrants ("Okies" from the Oklahoma dust bowl, "Arkies" from rural poverty in Arkansas) eventually wound up as a huge surplus labor force on the Pacific Coast. Some states, such as California, maintained a modest state work-camp program where migrants might find food, shelter, and work in local fields. Most, however, were forced to take jobs at a few cents a day on the great commercial farms of California, under conditions approaching peonage. Any attempt to organize on the migrants' part led to speedy repression.

While Midwestern farmers battled natural disaster, Southern tenant farmers and sharecroppers fought a losing fight against man-made disasters. The AAA programs, intended to raise the price of staple crops by cutting back production, paid money to *landowners*. But in the South, most of the actually farming labor was done by sharecroppers or tenant farmers, and since these did not own the land they worked, AAA benefits did not reach them. Quite the reverse. With a premium being placed on removing land from production, landowners found it profitable to drive their sharecroppers and tenants off the land.

Not that Southern agriculture had ever been less than savagely exploitive, long before the Depression. The sharecropper or tenant worked land not his own. He paid for the right to raise crops on the land, either by giving a share of the crops (50 per cent) or, if he were a tenant, by paying rent. Usually he had to be staked to seed, farm animals, tools, a shack, and even food. Usually the landowner advanced these, and, like workers in company towns, sharecroppers and tenants never seemed to earn enough to get out of debt to the landowner. Since tenants and "croppers" were usually illiterate, they had no means of checking the landowner's books anyhow.

Tenants and sharecroppers lived in a poverty which could only be measured against conditions in famine-stricken China or the poorest tribal villages of the Congo. Whole families worked in the fields from sun-up to sun-down. They lived in broken-down shanties without sanitation, plumbing, heating, or windows. Their food was sowbelly and weeds; their diseases were pellagra, malaria, and malnutrition; their death rate was fantastically high.

Most croppers earned less than $200 per year (which they never saw, of course, since they would owe it to the landowner or the landowner's store). In the early 1930's there were no less than eight and one half million people (of which little more than half were Negroes) living in these conditions as tenants or croppers in the South.

Driven to desperation, in July of 1934 Arkansas tenant farmers and sharecroppers (white and Negro together under Socialist leadership) formed the Southern Tenant Farmers' Union. The landowners responded with a campaign of terror. Posses hunted down union organizers as if they were slaves. Union members were flogged, beaten, and lynched, and their shanties burned. When Socialist leader Norman Thomas attempted to address an STFU meeting in Arkansas, he was beaten and ridden out of town on a rail by drunken landowners led by the sheriff. When Thomas brought reports of what was happening in the South to Roosevelt, he found the President sympathetic but unable to take action that might rouse Southern Congressmen against vital New Deal measures. "I know the South," Roosevelt told Thomas, "and there is arising a new generation of leaders in the South and we've got to be patient."

Nevertheless, in April, 1935, FDR set up the Resettlement Administration to begin to cope with the problems of rural poverty. Rexford Tugwell was named to head the new agency. Its program was to remove farmers (especially tenants and sharecroppers) from submarginal land and resettle them on good soil with government-supplied equipment and seed to give them a fresh start. The Resettlement Administration hoped to move 500,000 families, but it succeeded only in moving about 4,500, largely because it never received enough money. In 1937 Alabama Senator John Bankhead pushed through Congress (with FDR's blessing) a Farm Tenancy Act which created yet another new agency, the Farm Security Administration. The FSA loaned money to tenants and sharecroppers with which they could buy their own farms, and it helped the Midwestern migrants by establishing clean and sanitary, if austere, rest camps across the country where they might find refuge on their forlorn trek. By 1941 the FSA had spent nearly $1 billion in its various programs but had barely scratched the surface of Southern rural poverty. Southern land-owners combined with large Northern food processors and textile mills to oppose any basic change in the social structure of agri-culture. And while the millions of sharecroppers seldom voted and had few friends on Capitol Hill, the landowners and proces-sors spoke through many Senators and Congressmen. FSA was never given even a fraction of the funds necessary for it to come to grips with the deepest problems of rural poverty. These prob-lems were to remain to enrich a few, blight the lives of millions, and pose further serious problems for later generations.

Except for the provision of direct relief, there was little the New Deal could do for the displaced farmers of the Midwest. The AAA was being administered by state Farm Bureaus and Land Grant Colleges, themselves representative only of the richer farmers and the commercial farm interests and more and more deeply controlled by large insurance companies. And the AAA program itself was not geared to benefit the single-family farm. Government price support worked mainly to the benefit of the largest, mechanized farms, and these were often owned by food-processing companies or giant agricultural combines. Those "small" farmers who were able to maintain themselves with AAA help found themselves acting as a funnel for federal money which passed through their hands into the coffers of banks and insurance companies who owned the mortgages. Only by comparison with the crisis years of 1930 to 1933 could the lot of the small farmer be said to have improved. But as in industry so, too, in agriculture: with or without depressions, dust storms, or New Deal measures, the pressure of technological change was all towards consolida-tion of production and concentration of ownership. The small farmer could not compete economically with the giant com-mercial farms, except when he organized himself into cooperative associations. All during the 1930's the cooperative movement gained strength in the Midwest, especially in Minnesota and Iowa, despite harassment by food processors. Cooperatives found ready support in Washington from the New Deal, but this was a battle the farmers had to wage for themselves, by and large. Not until the 1940's would farmers' cooperatives emerge as a potent economic and political force.

But if Roosevelt felt his hands were tied in attempting to deal with rural poverty, and if there was nothing anyone could do about the tragedy of the dust bowl, there was much that could be done to prevent a recurrence of that disaster. FDR was himself an expert in soil conservation, both in theory and (on his Hyde Park farm) in practice. And in the Civilian Conservation Corps, with its hundreds of thousands of city boys transplanted to Western prairies and forests, he had a ready army with which to battle the dust bowl. The CCC boys, as has already been pointed out, built many of the smaller dams which held back streams and river branches, controlling the floods which had carried off the crumbling topsoil. They also, specifically at Roosevelt's insistence, planted a huge "shelterbelt" of trees which stretched from Canada to Abilene, Texas; over two hundred million trees were planted to break the winds, hold water in the soil, and hold the soil itself in place. Critics said it could not be done ("If God couldn't grow trees on the plains, the New Deal certainly can't!"), but it was done. One hundred miles deep and more than a thousand miles long, the great shelterbelt of trees took root and flourished. And, of course, many minor shelterbelts were planted across states and counties, too. They are, for the most part, flourishing there today, and so is the soil. Too late a program to help the sufferers of 1933 to 1936, the shelterbelts (and their complex supporting systems of dams, lakes, and national forests) ensure that no matter how severe or prolonged a drought may come to the Midwest in the future, the skies will never again blacken with dust.

An integral part of the soil conservation program was the education of farmers in anti-erosion tactics. Carried out through the Department of Agriculture and local county agents, this program taught farmers about crop rotation, strip farming, and how to "give the land a rest." The Soil Conservation Act of 1935 gave the federal government power to enforce conservation policies. Henceforth the land was to be considered a national estate which no man had the right to despoil for future generations. It would be years before the ravages of the dust storms could be repaired (in many areas they would never be repaired), and there would be decades of battle ahead between those who wanted to preserve the national domain and those whose drive for profits at any price led them to litter, pollute, and poison it. But the New Deal had created the atmosphere and some of the techniques through which conservation programs of the future could succeed. A time was coming, as Henry Wallace observed, when people would think of "this whole country as a good farmer thinks of his farm."

But soil conservation programs and remedial measures against rural poverty were, at best, defensive. FDR and the New Dealers had a broader vision of what they wanted to accomplish in the countryside, however. Nowhere was that vision brought nearer to reality than in the Tennessee Valley.

The basin of the Tennessee River and its tributaries drained parts of seven states: Tennessee, Alabama, Georgia, Mississippi, North Carolina, Kentucky, and Virginia. Streams spilled down from the Great Smokies and the Blue Ridge Mountains into the valleys below, uniting into larger rivers (the Holston, the French Broad) feeding into the Tennessee itself, which meandered for six hundred and fifty miles before it emptied into the Ohio. This was an area of forty thousand square miles, encompassing the forests of the Great Smokies, the rich cotton lands of Alabama, and the flat red soil of Georgia. But various as its physical surroundings were, the Tennessee flowed past one continuous condition—desperate poverty. Before the Civil War, the Tennessee Valley had supported a few great landowners and a mass of desperately poor people who scratched a living from marginal uplands. After the war, Northern businessmen came in to cut down the vast forests of the region and to exploit its gas and oil reserves. The land and the people who remained on it had been ruined. And to man's ravages, nature added yearly. Each year fifty-two inches of rain came to flood the rivers into torrents and carry off the topsoil.

The Tennessee Valley Authority had been created as one of the measures of the New Deal's first "hundred days." It created a federal agency which was to have control over dams, navigation, conservation, electrification, and community planning throughout the length and breadth of the Valley. Taking over the federally constructed dam and power station at Muscle Shoals for a starter (and thereby fulfilling the life's dream of Nebraska's great old progressive Senator George Norris), TVA was meant not only to build dams and generate electricity for the Valley inhabitants, not only to manufacture fertilizer and make the Tennessee River navigable, but to create an entire new life for the people who lived near it. By generating cheap power, it was hoped that light industry would be attracted to the Valley. This, combined with reclamation of the farming potential in the soil, would, it was hoped, bring to reality the New Deal dream of remaking the very quality of Valley life, by combining industry and agriculture in a harmonious balance which would bring the benefits of prosperity without blighting the lives of the people. Towns were to be rebuilt as model communities which combined the best of country and urban living. Schools, hospitals, roads, factories, farms were all to be created as part of an integrated plan, powered and nursed by the mighty but now-tamed river. So much for the dream.

From the very beginning, TVA found itself under powerful attack from the private electric power companies of the region. Wendell Willkie, the young, dynamic President of the Commonwealth and Southern Corporation (which controlled the Alabama, Georgia, and Tennessee public power utilities), led the assault. His first line of attack was that there was no market for the great amount of power TVA would generate in the Valley. There was but little industry there, and the local inhabitants could not afford domestic electricity (in fact, only two families out of every hundred in that huge area had any electric service at all). To this, TVA defenders responded by pointing out that

the march of time

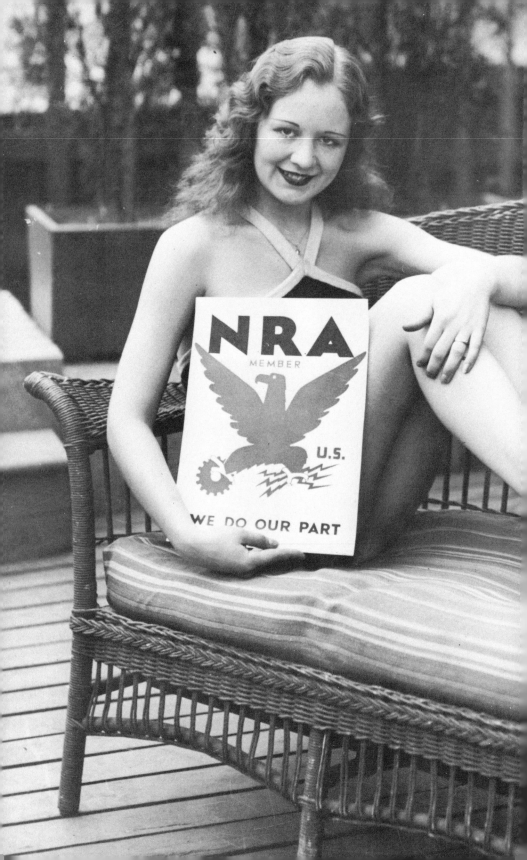

NRA was only a memory now—judged unconstitutional by the U.S. Supreme Court. But it had held the line for two vital years. Now labor was coming into its own—and the people were beginning to feel their strength.

The Congress of Industrial Organizations (CIO) was a going concern, and its first President, John L. Lewis, received congratulations on November 19, 1938, as he was preparing for new organizing drives.

In San Francisco, strikers were joined by WPA workers and officials to protest Congressional relief cuts—an unprecedented symbol of government-labor cooperation.

The Depression had by no means been licked. City slums remained to
fester and grow over the years ahead.

As did the signs of rural poverty. The hard core problems have never been faced.

Despite the good-will "tokenism" of Marian Anderson's appearance at the Lincoln Memorial (after the Daughters of the American Revolution had denied her the right to sing in their Constitution Hall) in 1939——

the problem of race relations was left as a fiery heritage for later generations to solve.

The explosion of the German dirigible *Hindenburg* at Lakehurst, New Jersey, in May, 1937, seemed to symbolize the breakdown in international relations which was diverting more and more attention from domestic problems.

There were many (including John L. Lewis (left), Senator Burton K. Wheeler (center), and Dr. Frank Townsend) who stumped the land preaching isolationism in 1939 and 1940. "Keep America Out of Europe's War" was the message.

But the approaching war meant jobs. The "Help Wanted" signs were going up again across the country.

And on Labor Day, 1940, the crowds watching parades in cities and towns throughout America were better dressed, better fed and more hopeful than they had been for a decade——

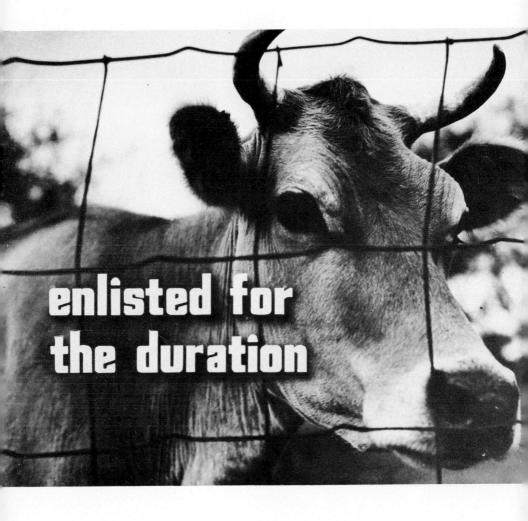

enlisted for
the duration

despite the growing drum rolls of approaching war.

the generation of power would inevitably attract an industrial market for it, and that the TVA program included provision for electrifying rural communities. Retreating, then, from the original objection, Willkie and the utilities interests declared that if the government were to generate power, then that power should be sold to the local private utilities companies who would in turn carry it over their own transmission lines and sell it for both commercial and private use. Anything else would be "Socialism," Willkie warned.

But it was the very failure of private utilities companies to bring electricity to the Valley's inhabitants (there was no profit in it) which had been one of the original reasons for setting up TVA. The idea that private companies were now to make profits out of federally constructed projects, paid for by the tax money of all Americans, was unacceptable.

TVA was administered by a board of three men. Chairman of the board was Arthur E. Morgan, President of Antioch College in Ohio and the man who had designed many an American flood-control project. He shared FDR's vision of TVA as an instrument to remake the total life of the Valley. "The improvement of that total well being, in physical, social and economic condition, is the total aim," he declared. To join him on the board, Roosevelt appointed Harcourt Morgan of Tennessee, an agricultural scientist, and young (he was thirty-four at the time) David E. Lilienthal, a Wisconsin lawyer specializing in utilities regulation who had helped draft the New Deal railroad regulation law. A man who put the public interest before all else, Lilienthal was an enthusiastic advocate of the potential of cheap and plentiful electric power. "We are just at the beginning of the power age," he remarked, "the future possibilities . . . are limitless."

Differences in emphasis soon produced differences of opinion over policy in the TVA board. Thus, Arthur Morgan wanted to see a revival of folk craft such as basket weaving among the Valley's inhabitants. But Lilienthal objected, observing, "We cannot prepare for the 'second coming of Daniel Boone' in a simple handicraft economy." But although he advocated industrialization of the Valley, Lilienthal was also determined that the entire TVA program should be carried out only in accordance with the freely expressed wishes of the people of the Valley. From the very start TVA decisions were to be submitted to local communities and groups for consultation, participation, and approval.

And as the years passed, something of a miracle took place in the Valley. Within ten years TVA built twenty-one dams, and the mighty power generated by the rivers of the Tennessee marched across the countryside on high steel towers, carried through gleaming copper cables to every corner of the land. Because TVA sold its power without profit, and sold it when possible to local cooperative societies and municipalities, its rates were very cheap. Industry did indeed begin to come to the Valley, and farmers' houses were now lighted. Electric appliances—from washing machines to pumps to farm equipment—began to relieve some of the burden of farm living. Because TVA's rates were low, local private power companies were forced to lower their rates also in order to compete. And despite the outcry of Commonwealth and Southern and their ilk, it was observed that broad new markets were thereby opened for private power, too. And the river itself, which had once foamed yellow and turbulent with the topsoil of the Valley, was now placid, blue, and navigable for large ships all the way to the Ohio. By 1956, two billion tons of freight would have moved along the river, through the TVA channels and locks. The dreary fastness of the mountain forests was now broken by sparkling lakes, stocked with fish by the Forestry Department, and set aside for public recreation. Under TVA leadership the agricultural methods of the Valley were transformed. Broad belts of trees were planted to fight soil erosion; millions of acres of farmland were replanted with crops such as clover and alfalfa, which rebuilt soil strength; over a million acres were terraced. New roads brought new life to old towns, new industries brought new towns to the countryside. Richer tax yields brought new schools and hospitals and public services. And the lives of the people of the Valley—even if they were not transformed to the extent originally hoped for by the New Dealers— were transformed beyond all the expectations of TVA's critics.

"TVA," said Congressman John Rankin, "is the most profitable investment the American people have made since the Louisiana Purchase."

Although TVA was the nation's only valley authority, it was by no means the only government-sponsored public power project. Bonneville Dam and the colossal Grand Coulee Dam brought the waters of the Columbia River under control and supplied tremendous amounts of cheap power to the burgeoning Northwest. Boulder Dam on the Colorado River (started under the administration of Herbert Hoover but transformed and completed by the New Deal) brought water and energy to parts of Nevada and California. There were hundreds of other projects— some built by PWA, some by WPA, and some by the Army engineers. Almost all the projects were criticized as being wasteful: who would use all that new energy? And the outcry against government invasion of the private power industry never diminished over the years and can be heard today. But this running argument was but a part of a larger debate. Some Americans held that under a system of free enterprise, the resources of the country ought to be privately owned and privately developed. Only the motive of profit, it has been held, could assure rapid, efficient development in the eventual best interests of all the people. Other Americans held that the country and its natural resources belonged to all the people and were not to be developed for the benefit of private interests. Rapid, efficient development would be motivated by a clear national understanding of national needs on the part of the people, financed by their taxes and directed by their elected government in their own best interests. The argument has still to be resolved.

In one sense, TVA's critics were correct at first: with all this new power spreading over the land, who was going to buy it? Private utilities companies had found it unprofitable to transmit power to the countryside because farmers simply couldn't afford to pay for it. In 1935 most of America was blacked out at night. Power and light ended at town and city limits; beyond, the roads curved away into darkness. As early as 1933, FDR had set up committees to study the problems of rural electrification. By 1935 funds for a Rural Electrification Administration were voted by Congress as part of the emergency relief measure of that year. On May 11, 1935, the REA, under the chairmanship of Morris Cooke, an old fighter for public power, went to work.

Cooke tried at first to enlist the cooperation of private power companies, but the companies would not cooperate in a program they viewed as both unnecessary and a threat to their very existence. Utilities companies fought REA by attempting to rush power lines into the most potentially profitable areas and, more importantly, by bringing massive lawsuits against the new agency as "unconstitutional" in its basis and in its operations. REA responded to these tactics by lending its large funds to farmers' cooperatives and to local municipalities to enable them to pay for new generating plants of their own and the building of transmission lines from federally owned dams. Although REA was willing to lend money to private groups, as part of its program, preference always went to non-profit agencies. Despite court injunctions, local obstructionist tactics on the part of private power companies, and the low income of depression-struck farmers, REA got the job done. In 1934 only one out of every ten American farms had electricity; by 1950, nine out of every ten.

New Deal measures did not end depression in the countryside. As late as 1939, little groups of migrants from Midwestern dust bowls or Southern poverty could be seen huddled around their broken-down cars outside gas stations on the roads that led westward. And farm prices, although they rose dramatically over their 1930 lows, never reached prosperous levels until the Second World War created a new demand for food in abundance. Nor did New Deal laws automatically save the countryside from erosion and man-made disaster; the current debate over water and air pollution amply demonstrates that this fight will continue for many years. But the New Deal did make a start towards reform and did establish guidelines for policies which were eventually to transform both the countryside and the men who wrested a living from it.

ten The Rise of Labor

Rush, says the boss,
Work like a hoss;
I'll take the profits and you take the loss,
I've got the brains, I've got the dough
The Lord Himself decreed it so.

CIO Strike Song

When they tie the can to a union man,
    Sit down! Sit down!
When they give him the sack, they'll take him back,
    Sit down! Sit down!
When the boss won't talk, don't take a walk,
    Sit down! Sit down!

UAW Strike Song

IT WAS very much a singing movement. That was part of an older heritage of work songs transformed into militant hymns by such bygone groups as the Knights of Labor and the International Workers of the World. Some of the songs were devised as the simplest means of teaching union principles to semi-literate workers in Southern textile mills or Pennsylvania coal fields. Others were meant to instill courage in strikers faced with battalions of hired thugs or the National Guard. The greatest of all American anthems, Julia Ward Howe's "Battle Hymn of the Republic," was given new words:

They have taken untold millions, that they never toiled to earn,
But without our brain and muscle, not a single wheel could turn;

We can break their haughty power, gain our freedom when we
learn—
 That the Union makes us strong.
 Solidarity forever,
 Solidarity forever,
 Solidarity forever,
 For the Union makes us strong!

Yet in 1932 there were few signs of new militancy in the American labor movement. For more than ten years, unionism had been in a steady decline. In 1920, about 12 per cent of all American workers were members of unions; by 1932 only 6 per cent belonged. Furthermore, the American Federation of Labor, the federation of hundreds of local skilled craft unions, showed little promise of offering any positive leadership towards new goals. But under the impact of depression, and with the coming of the New Deal, the workers themselves, both organized and unorganized, were demonstrating a new and grim determination to win a better place for themselves in the national economy. In 1933, three times as many workers went out on strike as in 1932. Taxi drivers struck in New York, shipyard workers in New Jersey, aluminum workers in Pennsylvania, copper miners in Montana. And in 1934 there were even more strikes. Perhaps of greater importance, the nature of the strikes had changed. In the past, with or without the somnolent leadership of the conservative AFL, workers had struck for higher wages or better conditions; in 1934 they were striking for the right to organize themselves into new unions. So vital was this right to workers, and so hateful to employers, that many industries, many cities, witnessed something like small-scale civil war during the thirties.

The AFL, cleaving to the advice of its founder, Samuel Gompers, had concentrated on organizing unions only among the skilled workers. Thus there were unions of carpenters, machinists, coal miners, typographers, railroad engineers. They were not organized by industry, but by the nature of their particular skill or craft. Considered unskilled, and hence beyond the pale of AFL organizing activities, were those such as steel workers, auto workers, and truck drivers. Thus the overwhelming majority of American workers were excluded from the AFL by its own policies. But with growing labor discontent building up dangerous pressure in 1933 and 1934, AFL policy began to change. By 1935, conservative AFL President William Green told a Congressional committee: " . . . the spirit of the workers in America has been aroused. They are going to find a way to bargain collectively. . . . Labor must have its place in the sun."

One of the immediate causes of the new militancy of labor was that section of the NRA which called upon employers to set minimum wages and maximum hours, abolish child labor, and allow workers to organize into unions of their own choosing. Although in agreeing to NRA codes industrialists paid lip service to this section, they soon made it perfectly clear that they had no intention of seriously abiding by its provisions. If labor wanted its "place in the sun," it would have to fight for it. And workers were ready to fight.

Open industrial warfare commenced in Minneapolis in 1934. There, with the encouragement of Minnesota's Farmer-Labor Party Governor Floyd B. Olson, the truck drivers had begun to organize in 1933. Distribution and transportation were Minneapolis' life blood, and the city's businessmen, organized into a Citizens' Alliance, viewed the truck driver-organizing drive as an attempt to strangle the city. Despite the labor provisions of NRA, the Alliance refused to deal with the Teamsters' Union, and the truck drivers struck. On May 22, 1934, armed businessmen and special deputies clashed with workers in downtown Minneapolis. At this "Battle of Deputies Run," the businessmen suffered a defeat (two deputies were killed). Governor Olson called out the National Guard. Employers and workers began talking again, but the employers, still hoping to break the union, stopped talking in July. Once again the city was strikebound. The police decided to provoke action. They sent out a scab truck with an armed escort. When strikers tried to halt the truck, the police opened fire with pistols, rifles, and shotguns. In ten minutes they shot sixty-seven people, of whom two died. At the funeral of the victims, thousands and thousands of workers marched behind the coffins. Governor Olson proclaimed martial law and raided both Union and

Alliance headquarters impartially. Finally, on August 21, the Citizens' Alliance agreed to recognize the Teamsters' Union. At the cost of several dead, scores wounded, a four-month work stoppage, and hatreds which would last many years, the businessmen gave the workers what they had asked for in the first place.

1934 was also the year of the San Francisco strike when, for a moment, it seemed that open-class warfare had finally reached America. The great port city had always had a brutal labor relations record. Merchant seamen were among the most heavily exploited of all American workers. When he was threatened with arrest for attempting to organize a union, sailor Andrew Furuseth replied, "You can put me in jail. But you cannot give me narrower quarters than as a seaman I have always had. You cannot give me coarser food than I have always eaten. You cannot make me lonelier than I have always been." Equally bitter were San Francisco's longshoremen, whose lives were made up of foggy mornings waiting on the piers for the "shape-up," a system to select the day's work force which was nothing more than brutal extortion on the part of gangster straw bosses, with an employers' blacklist for those who tried to fight back. Their leader was Harry Bridges, an Australian who had been both seaman and longshoreman, and who had lived in San Francisco since 1920. Bridges refused to say whether or not he was a Communist, and the seamen and dockers didn't care as long as he fought for them. When the NRA came to San Francisco, Bridges organized a local of the International Longshoremen's Association, and, when employers refused to recognize it, he led his men out on strike on May 9, 1934.

From the very first, violence broke out. When police tried to break the ILA picket lines, San Francisco's teamsters went out on strike in sympathy. As employers remained obdurate, the dock strike spread along the Pacific Coast to Seattle. On July 3, the local businessmen, organized into an "Industrial Association," tried to open the port of San Francisco by force. Trucks full of scabs, with police escorts, charged down upon the Embarcadero, and for days the port of San Francisco was a scene of fighting between pickets and scabs. On July 5, the police and special deputies used their guns, killing two workers and wounding many more. The National Guard marched in to restore order. "Bloody Thursday," as July 5 came to be known, united San Francisco's workers in bitter anger. On July 16, a general strike was proclaimed throughout the entire city. With the exception of essential services such as water, electricity, milk for children, and communications, all industrial life in San Francisco came to an end. San Francisco's business community thought the revolution had finally arrived. The city's mayor demanded federal troops to put an end to "insurrection." West Coast governors showered telegrams upon President Roosevelt demanding speedy and violent action. "Everybody demanded," FDR later recalled, "that I sail into San Francisco Bay, all flags flying, guns double-shotted, and end the strike. They went completely off the handle." But Roosevelt refused to intervene. He, like Labor Secretary Frances Perkins, did not view the general strike as the beginning of revolution but as labor's attempt to win recognition by the only means left open. Four days after it had started, the strike came to an end. The ILA agreed to accept arbitration and, in the end, won most of its demands.

Violence flared during the summer of 1934 in Toledo, Ohio, and in Kohler, Wisconsin. It was the same story: labor attempting to organize, local businessmen and deputies replying by violence, riots, shootings, dead and wounded workers, and, finally, recognition of a union, or uneasy armed truce.

By October, 1935, NRA had been declared unconstitutional and the National Labor Relations Board had been established to secure some of the gains workers had been promised under NRA. Organizational drives in such basic mass-production industries as automobiles, steel, and rubber had failed under conservative and somewhat less than militant AFL leadership. And in that month, the AFL national convention met in Atlantic City. A fight broke out immediately between the conservatives, headed by AFL President William Green, and a radical group who demanded immediate organization of unskilled, mass-production industries, led by John L. Lewis, President of the United Mine Workers Union. Arguments were bitter. The conservatives won a floor vote of the delegates against Lewis' position. Tempers grew short and wound up with Lewis knocking down "Big Bill" Hutcheson, President of the Carpenters' Union. Later, at a private meeting, Lewis, Phil Murray (also of UMW), Sidney Hillman and David Dubinsky of the garment workers, Max Zaritsky of the hatters, and Thomas McMahon of the textile workers formed a new Committee on Industrial Organization to act with or without AFL approval. The following year, the breach became official. Lewis' committee changed its name to the Congress of Industrial Organizations, and long years of factional strife in the ranks of labor began.

John Llewellyn Lewis, born in 1880 and President of the United Mine Workers since 1920, brought driving energy and an eloquence inherited from his Welsh ancestors to the fight to organize industrial workers. He knew from first-hand experience how bitter a worker's life could be and how brutally employers would fight to retain their ancient privileges. He had followed a conservative course during the twenties and had seen his own union dwindle to half its strength in the process. Depression and the New Deal fired him to more radical action. "The time has passed, in America," Lewis warned, "when the workers can be either clubbed, gassed or shot down with impunity. I solemnly warn the leaders of industry that labor will not tolerate such policies or tactics." Into the CIO ranks filed many of the ablest labor leaders. Some were ex-Socialists like Hillman and Dubinsky and Walter Reuther (who was struggling to organize auto workers in Detroit); some were Communists like Lee Pressman who left his New Deal job to become CIO General Counsel. Lewis did not particularly care what political beliefs a man held, provided he was devoted to labor's cause. Communists made good organizers—they were fired with faith, tireless, and, for the most part, fearless. Besides, John L. Lewis was used to controlling men, and he knew he could handle Communists or any other political extremists. "Who gets the bird," Lewis liked to ask, "the dog or the hunter?" Preparing for the harsh struggles ahead, Lewis declared, "Let the workers organize. Let the toilers assemble. Let their crystallized voice proclaim their injustices and demand their privileges. Let all thoughtful citizens sustain them, for the future of labor is the future of America."

And the struggles came. A Steel Workers' Organizing Committee had been established under the leadership of Lewis' United Mine Workers' lieutenant, Phil Murray. All through the early months of 1936, hundreds of organizers invaded the big steel plants. They were financed largely from UMW funds. Within twelve months they had organized more than 100,000 steel workers. The big steel companies fought back with every tactic they could find—labor spies, labor informers, thugs, special deputies, and advertisements attempting to raise public opinion against the workers. But just when a nationwide steel strike seemed all but inevitable, the Chairman of the Board of United States Steel, the country's largest steel producer, announced that the United Steel Workers Union had been recognized. Furthermore, steel workers won a 10 per cent wage increase and the forty-hour week. Other of the big steel companies quickly followed U.S. Steel's lead, but the "little" steel companies continued to hold out. These companies—Republic Steel, Bethlehem Steel, and Youngstown Sheet and Tube Company—determined to resort to force. The United Steel Workers Union called a strike against their plants in the spring of 1937, and 75,000 workers laid down their tools and walked out. The steel companies called in their thugs as usual to break picket lines, and violence flared in Pennsylvania, Ohio, and Illinois.

On Memorial Day in South Chicago, three hundred steel workers made a peaceful "protest" march. Police, without any provocation whatever, opened fire on them. The workers fled, but left ten of their number dead in the street and more than a hundred wounded behind. The police suffered none but minor injuries. The "Memorial Day Massacre" aroused public sympathy for the strikers across the country, but not in the company-owned,

company-policed, and company-controlled steel towns. Organized violence and organized propaganda on the part of the "little
steel" companies won in 1937. The strike was broken. Not until
1941 would "little steel" be organized through the intervention
of the federal government acting through the National Labor
Relations Board. By then the United Steel Workers had grown to
600,000 members. The blood on the consciences of the owners
and corporate directors of "little steel" won them just four years
of immunity from the inevitable.

While the steel workers were fighting, automobile workers in
Detroit under the leadership of Walter Reuther and his brother
were attempting to establish the United Automobile Workers
Union. The large auto manufacturers—General Motors, Chrysler, and Ford—refused to recognize the new union, despite the
provisions of the National Labor Relations Act. Open warfare
came when General Motors flatly refused to deal with the workers' representatives on any basis whatsoever. In January, 1937,
100,000 auto workers struck General Motors plants. But this time
a new tactic was introduced. The workers in some of the GM
plants—especially at Flint, Michigan—did not walk out. Instead
they sat down. They remained at their benches in the plants and
declared they would neither go back to work nor leave the plants
until they had won recognition. The brilliance of the "sit-down"
strike was at once apparent. General Motors, despite the fact
that it called for police and the National Guard to evict the workers from its property, did not dare to wage open warfare—that
would have ruined the plants. And with friends and relatives
bringing them food and supplies, the workers were prepared to sit
down indefinitely. When the police tried to rush one plant they
were met with a hail of pop bottles, iron bolts, and automobile
door hinges, and forced to retreat. Returning to the attack with
tear-gas bombs, they were driven back when the workers turned
the plant's high-powered fire hoses on them. It was now clear that
industrial plants made excellent fortresses.

Frustrated on the local level, General Motors obtained a court
injunction for the ejection of the workers as trespassers on private

property. The company called on Michigan Governor Frank Murphy to use the National Guard. The workers' leaders wired Murphy: "We the workers, have carried on a stay-in strike over a month to make General Motors Corporation obey the law and engage in collective bargaining . . . Unarmed as we are, the introduction of the militia, sheriffs or police with murderous weapons will mean a blood-bath of unarmed workers . . . We have decided to stay in the plant." As zero hour for the enforcement of the court injunction approached, thousands of friends and sympathizers with the workers' cause assembled outside the plants. They sang "Solidarity Forever" and prepared for battle. Governor Murphy, with Roosevelt's wholehearted support, refused to order in the militia. Instead he called officials of both General Motors and the United Automobile Workers to Detroit and forced them to negotiate. In the end, General Motors had to recognize the UAW, and Chrysler and others followed suit. Only Ford held out, but four years later, after bloodshed, bitterness, and growing public exasperation at Ford policy, that company too capitulated.

The success of the auto workers' sit-down technique led to a wave of sit-down strikes in 1937. Hundreds of thousands of men and women in the new unions—textile workers, rubber workers, janitors, department store clerks, electricians—sat down. Some cried that the technique, by invading the property rights of ownership, was completely opposed to the American way. Others pointed out that if sit-down strikes were technically illegal, so was management's refusal to abide by the terms of the National Labor Relations Act. Upton Sinclair declared that "For seventy-five years big business has been sitting down on the American people, and now I am delighted to see the process reversed." But when, finally, the Supreme Court found the National Labor Relations Act constitutional (and hence enforceable on management), the need for such tactics evaporated and sit-down strikes came to an end.

By the end of 1937, the CIO had built a total membership of 3,700,000. It had been successful in steel, in autos, in textiles, in rubber, in the great mass-production industries which had long been abandoned by the AFL. It had established the principle of organizing workers according to industries rather than according to their individual skills. It had organized unskilled workers by the hundreds of thousands. And it had stoutly enforced a democratic policy against discrimination. All classes and kinds of workers were, for the first time, welcomed into CIO unions—women, immigrants, and Negroes were accorded full and equal rights.

CIO success forced new policies on the AFL. Now the old craft unions began to accept unskilled members, and the federation even began to grant charters to new industrial unions. Soon there was active rivalry between CIO and AFL organizers in many industries. Attempts to bring about a reconciliation between the two national organizations repeatedly foundered on the rocks of personal antagonisms. Nevertheless, more and more the two rivals were pursuing the same policies, and as CIO membership rose, AFL membership kept pace. By the end of the decade, the CIO and AFL unions counted a membership of 10 million.

Franklin Roosevelt had had little experience with the problems of organized labor. He could bring to it none of the rich background he enjoyed in conservation, for example. But his instincts were generally on the side of working men—except for brief lapses. One such lapse, which occasioned a memorable exchange, occurred in 1937 during the critical days of the steel strikes. Confounded by a flood of urgent and contradictory advice, helpless to act directly in the situation, Roosevelt had petulantly exclaimed, "A plague on both your houses!" to labor and management. John L. Lewis replied: "It ill behooves one who has supped at labor's table and who has been sheltered in labor's house to curse with equal fervor and fine impartiality both labor and its adversaries when they become locked in deadly embrace."

Roosevelt certainly had supped at labor's table. Not only did the CIO and the UMW contribute close to $740,000 to the Democratic war chest in 1936, but through such organizations as the CIO Political Action Committee, organized in towns and cities throughout the country, labor leaders had worked mightily to get out the labor vote for Roosevelt. While labor had to fight its own battles, the New Deal program included vital measures that would benefit workers. As Lewis explained, ". . . industries may be unionized, but, on the other hand, better living standards, shorter working hours and improved economic conditions for their members cannot be hoped for unless legislative or other provisions be made for economic planning and for price, production and profit controls."

It was not surprising that labor should support the New Deal. What was surprising was that labor did not attempt to form its own political party, as it had succeeded in doing in England. But except for the establishment of the state American Labor Party in New York, the unions avoided third-party activity. The American labor movement, to the incredulity and disgust of its European counterparts, had always been non-political. It had always concentrated on winning higher wages, shorter hours—on improvements in the immediate and daily life of its members— rather than on an attempt to win political power. There were several possible reasons for this. First of all, a political labor party would have admitted the existence of a laboring class—that is, a class of workers conscious of itself as a class, willing to organize to win its class interests. But class consciousness was not part of the American workers' heritage. Except in the South, the United States had never known a rigid class society. There were no feudal hangovers or aristocratic cobwebs to be swept away when the industrial revolution reached America during the Civil War. In times of depression, for many decades the Western frontier acted as a safety valve, drawing off the more desperate and the more resolute who might have led the fight for better conditions back East. Secondly, although conservatives and industrialists might fight them every step of the way, workers had reason to believe that they could change their conditions through political action as American voters, rather than as working-class rebels. Reform was slow, painfully slow—but it did take place. When conditions became too terrible, partly out of fear, partly out of a realization that justice ought to prevail in theory at least, society made concessions. Workers' votes could be potent ammunition in America. Finally, workers were no more immune to the "American dream" than any other segment of the American people. They too had been raised in a capitalistic society, in a free society of law. They believed in the same virtues of thrift, honesty, and hard work as businessmen and, more importantly, believed like everyone else that these virtues would bring material rewards under the capitalistic system of private enterprise. To have organized a separate labor party would have meant acknowledging that they were indeed "outside" society, a different class, a different kind of Americans. It would have meant giving up the dream, and through hard times and good, workers clung to it.

Yet the Great Depression was teaching lessons. It was teaching that if workers did not consider themselves a separate class, many businessmen thought of them that way. It was teaching that the old virtues by no means guaranteed survival, much less "success." Class consciousness and class warfare came as close to being a valid definition of American society during the Great Depression as ever in American history—but not quite close enough. The prime reason that the Depression's bitter lessons did not lead to a political cleavage along class lines in America was, without doubt, the existence of the New Deal. By incorporating so many immediate reforms within the corpus of one of the two major political parties, the New Deal drew off the lightning of rebellion.

There would come a time when union men were hardly distinguishable from businessmen, a time when union headquarters looked like the head offices of giant corporations, a time when union leaders, under pressure from those who were once their mortal enemies, would turn on some of the most selfless of their organizers as "Reds," a time when big unions would sit side by side with big businesses to maintain a conservative status quo. But that time was not yet. The Depression years were rather the time of freezing hours on picket lines, the time of rocks and bottles and bullets, the time of solidarity and enthusiasm, a time of singing as if you meant it.

eleven Stalemate, Recession, and the Steady Drummer

A judge is a law student who grades his own papers.
H. L. Mencken

We hunt the cause of ruin, add,
Subtract, and put ourselves in pawn;
For all our scratching on the pad,
We cannot trace the error down.
Theodore Roethke

It takes a long, long time to bring the past
up to the present.
Franklin D. Roosevelt

ROOSEVELT'S SECOND inaugural address, on January 20, 1937, had included the memorable lines: "I see one-third of a nation ill-housed, ill-clad, ill-nourished." And as the New Deal's second term opened to the subsiding of Midwestern dust clouds and the increasing din of industrial warfare, the problem of hard-bed poverty in America seemed no nearer to a solution than it had been four years earlier. But with an overwhelming victory at the polls behind him, FDR determined to do battle with that segment of the government which had, as he saw it, steadily opposed all measures of relief and reform: the United States Supreme Court.

The "nine old men" had, in the spring of 1936, struck down the NRA and the AAA as unconstitutional. New measures had been hastily passed to secure most AAA provisions, and the Wagner Act had at least attempted to preserve labor's new-won rights from the wreckage of NRA. But the Court seemed to go out of its way a month later to rule that New York State's minimum-wage law was invalid and the federal Coal Conservation Act unconstitutional. The conservative majority on the Court seemed determined that no legislation would be allowed in the broad field of economic control. Its decisions suggested that the vital Wagner Act would not survive a court test.

There was no holier cow on the American landscape than the Supreme Court. It was viewed by most Americans as an august, all-but-divine assembly of men far above political strife who guarded the shrine of the American Constitution much as ancient Rome's vestal virgins guarded the shrine of that earlier republic's gods. People had long since forgotten that the Supreme Court could, from time to time, reveal itself as all too human and prone to human error. Forgotten was the infamous Dred Scott decision which had declared the Negro to be beyond the pale of human rights and helped provoke the Civil War. Forgotten, too, were the battles which former Presidents such as Jefferson, Jackson, and Lincoln had waged against the Court. To tamper with the Supreme Court seemed, to all but a few Americans, much like monkeying around with the Holy Bible.

On February 5, 1937, Roosevelt sent to Congress a proposal to redesign the federal judiciary. He declared that a deficiency in judges had resulted in overcrowding the courts' dockets. Furthermore, aged or infirm judges could not handle the amount of work now pouring down upon them. He proposed that if *any* federal judge, having served ten years, refused to resign after his seventieth birthday, the President be empowered to appoint a new judge to the bench, including, if circumstances required, six new judges to the Supreme Court. The idea had been "packaged" by Attorney General Homer Cummings, but it had originated many years before in the mind of none other than arch conservative Supreme Court Justice James McReynolds himself.

The uproar was immediate and fierce. The "Court-packing bill," as FDR's proposal was called, united Democrats and Republicans in opposition. Many men in and out of Congress who hated the New Deal but had feared to oppose its economic policies for fear of popular reprisal at the polls, now seized upon the Court bill as a rallying point around which to unite. Hatton Summers, Chairman of the House Judiciary Committee, told his colleagues, "Boys, here's where I cash in my chips." Letters and telegrams rained on Congress from a broad cross section of Americans, all urging resistance to the new bill. And, of vital importance, New Deal Senators and those Republican progressives who had supported FDR's program joined the chorus of criticism. Senator Norris asked himself how he would have felt if "Harding had offered this bill." For, if liberals were generally prepared to trust Roosevelt's discretion, they were certainly not prepared to pass a law which would enable future Presidents, who might or might not share FDR's views, to pack the Supreme Court, the nation's last refuge against unjust laws.

Roosevelt had expected opposition. He felt he had no choice but to do something about Supreme Court obstructionism and thereby hand his enemies an issue around which they could unite. But he was unprepared for the opposition his proposal earned from New Dealers and liberals. He also underestimated the power of the Court itself to affect popular opinion. On March 29, 1937, the Supreme Court upheld the validity of a Washington State minimum-wage law similar to the New York statute it had struck down a short time before. Two weeks later the Court found the Wagner Act constitutional. By these decisions the Court reversed itself and let much of the steam out of its critics' boilers. Then, on May 18, 1937, aged conservative Justice Willis Van Devanter announced his retirement. This would give FDR the chance to appoint a liberal justice and thereby ensure a Court majority in favor of New Deal legislation. Van Devanter's retirement was followed by a letter from Chief Justice Charles

Evans Hughes to Senator Burton K. Wheeler in which the Chief Justice succinctly and devastatingly obliterated Roosevelt's arguments about inefficiency in the Supreme Court. FDR's proposals, Hughes pointed out, would only result in "more judges to hear, more judges to confer, more judges to discuss, more judges to be convinced and to decide." Hughes' blast was followed in turn by a Supreme Court verdict which declared the Social Security Act constitutional.

It was perfectly apparent that at last here was a political battle FDR was going to lose. His closest supporters in Congress begged him to withdraw his proposal. But the President's dander was up and he stuck by his guns. Not until July 22, 1937, after the Democratic Party had torn itself to shreds over the bill and even such arch New Dealers as New York's Governor Herbert Lehman had come out against it, did Roosevelt give in. His proposal was "recommitted for further study," and that was the end of it—almost.

In later years Roosevelt was to claim he had lost the Supreme Court battle but won the war. He evidently felt that his "court-packing" proposal had forced the Supreme Court to adopt more liberal attitudes. That was debatable, but coincidence, at least, was on FDR's side of the argument. The old adage that the Supreme Court "follows the election returns" was probably, in part at least, true. Certainly the battle forced justices to rethink their opinions and responsibilities. In any event, in the years immediately following the court battle, FDR was able to appoint five new justices, thereby ensuring the survival of his program.

But in a larger sense, Roosevelt may well have lost the war. For the Supreme Court bill destroyed the unity of the Democratic party and the unity of the Democratic-Republican progressive alliance in Congress. Using the Supreme Court bill as a rallying point, a new coalition was beginning to form on Capitol Hill. It was a coalition of conservative Republicans and Southern Democrats who felt, for particular reasons, that the New Deal had gone far enough. The entire New Deal program was, of course, anathema to conservatives. But it was now also frightening some liberals. They feared that the power of Big Government was replacing the power of Big Business. Southerners feared the social implications of AAA measures in the South, and detested Roosevelt's friendliness to the cause of Negro rights. Many middle-class Americans were now becoming frightened, too, by the growing power of the unions. Also, there was a general feeling that the time of crisis was past, that the country deserved a breather from new legislation. Thus, in a sense, the very success of the New Deal contributed to strengthening its enemies. By the spring of 1937, the country had finally pulled above the production, profit, and wage levels of 1929. The pressure was off, the problems were solved or on their way to solution, and people were tired of fervor.

Then, in August, 1937, disaster struck again. The economy suddenly tumbled. Industrial output fell overnight in the most dramatic drop in American history—worse even than the downfall of 1930. All the gains of the past were wiped out. In three months steel production fell from 80 per cent of capacity to 19 per cent. Once again the stock market plunged. And by January 1, 1938, more than two million people had been thrown out of work.

As FDR had been willing to take credit for recovery, so now he had to shoulder responsibility for what his enemies gleefully called the "Roosevelt recession." And, in truth, the President had contributed to it. The prosperity of 1937 had been built upon shaky foundations. There were still seven million unemployed, and only by government deficit spending—the pouring of gigantic sums of money into the economy through relief and public works —had the semblance of prosperity been achieved. But in June of 1937, attacked once again by a wave of worry about government debt and spending, and urged by some advisors to try to balance the federal budget, Roosevelt had slashed spending to the bone. He had cut WPA rolls drastically and slowed PWA projects to a standstill. This might not have had an adverse effect on the economy if private business had been ready or able to resume investment and expansion, but in 1937 private business was still not ready to do so. Many businessmen simply had lost confidence in the economy, many more feared New Deal policies, and a few held back in a conscious effort to discredit the administration. In cutting spending Roosevelt had jovially referred to taking off "the bandages and throwing away the crutches" to see if the patient could walk. The patient collapsed.

Many New Dealers had been opposed to the cutback in spending. Aside from those like Hopkins and Ickes who did not like to see their own programs diminished, there were important economists who felt that it was a dangerous policy. Marriner Eccles, Governor of the Federal Reserve Board, expressed it succinctly. "Government," he declared, "must be the compensatory agent in this economy; it must unbalance its budget, [spend] during deflation [when private spending sank] and create surpluses [save] during periods of great business activity."

While the argument raged, once again, in early 1938, many Americans came close to starvation. In Chicago, children were digging through garbage cans again; in Cleveland people fought over rotten vegetables in the streets; in the Midwest generally WPA rolls increased by 200 per cent in six months. Cities such as Omaha, Toledo, and Chicago were once again running out of relief funds (Chicago closed down all nineteen of its relief stations). By April, 1938, the roll of the unemployed stood once again at ten million, and conservative critics of the New Deal were all but dancing in the street. The people's disaster, by seeming to prove the New Deal wrong, gladdened their hearts. And, after staving off the dire necessity as long as possible, on April 2, 1938, Roosevelt caved in and sent a new large-scale spending program to Congress. He asked for, and received, a total of $3.75 billion, to be split up between PWA, WPA, and various relief agencies. Thereafter the economy began to recover.

Hard hit during the 1938 recession had been farmers. The AAA had been declared unconstitutional in 1936, and, as has been pointed out, many of its provisions were unworkable anyhow, while others only increased misery in the South. Henry Wallace had long had a vision of an "ever-normal granary." Like Joseph in the Old Testament, he wanted the government to buy and store surplus crops during times of overproduction against times of famine and want. In February, 1938, Congress (now all but out of FDR's control) passed a new AAA bill which went far towards satisfying farmers' demands. It authorized crop loans, crop insurance against natural disasters, and large subsidies to farmers who agreed to cut back production. It also made acreage allotments enforceable under law. As Senator Charles McNary pointed out, it made "the Secretary of Agriculture the autocrat of the breakfast table." No provisions were adopted to come to grips with the problems of sharecroppers, to dig into the root causes of rural poverty. The new AAA bill, while better than nothing, was obviously intended to give organized and relatively well-off farmers a permanent draft on the U. S. Treasury, at the taxpayers' expense. By 1939, with farmers still overproducing and with AAA pouring money into farm-subsidy programs, the essential problem of a healthy farm economy in a capitalistic society had still not been solved. Only the onset of war and the subsequent great demand for food relieved the federal government from disbursing huge sums of money taken from most American taxpayers to support other Americans who happened to be farmers.

The new coalition of conservative Republicans and Southern Democrats represented, by and large, Northern business interests and Southern landowners. The businessmen were united by fear of labor unions, uneasiness over rapidly mounting federal deficits, and, among the more rabid, a blind and unreasoning hatred of the man with whom they associated their downfall. Southerners, on the other hand, had largely supported New Deal measures which were bitterly opposed by businessmen. Their growing opposition to Roosevelt was based on fear that the New Deal, by advancing social legislation, would undermine the rigid race structure of the South, thereby undermining an economic autocracy as well. If ever the Negroes and poor whites of the South united to fight for economic liberty, then the rule of landowners and big business, along with their rabble-rousing political front men, would come to an end.

Although neither Roosevelt nor his administration had any

fixed policy towards Negroes, they were determined to help the poor, among whom Negroes bulked large. No discrimination was permitted in any of the government relief programs, and direct orders went out that a certain percentage of Negroes had to be employed in administering such programs as PWA. Negro educator Mary McLeod Bethune directed a Negro Affairs Division in the WPA. On the other hand, when an anti-lynching bill was proposed in Congress in 1936, Roosevelt did not feel able to give it all-out support for fear of arousing Southern Senators to opposition against vital New Deal reform measures. Negroes, the first fired and the last hired, suffered more from the Depression than any other class of Americans and therefore had more reason to appreciate New Deal relief and reform laws. And the New Deal brought Negroes symbolic victories, too. Roosevelt appointed eminent Negroes such as Robert C. Weaver and William H. Hastie to government posts, kept his office open to consultations with leaders such as Walter White of the NAACP and W. E. B. DuBois. When, in 1939, the Daughters of the American Revolution refused permission for Negro opera star Marian Anderson to sing in Constitution Hall, Mrs. Roosevelt canceled her membership in that organization and, with FDR's blessing, organized a mammoth audience of 25,000 to hear Marian Anderson sing on the steps of the Lincoln Memorial. The popularity of Roosevelt with Negroes was such that an estimated 80 per cent of Negro voters cast their ballots for him in 1936 and 1940. Southern conservatives had reason indeed to fear the import of the New Deal for race relations.

The new Northern conservative-Southern alliance in Congress was not strong enough in April, 1938, to prevent the passage of the Fair Labor Standards Act of that year. But it was strong enough to so load it down with amendments that it turned out a far from satisfactory measure. Originally designed to preserve in law some of the provisions of the now defunct NRA codes, the Fair Labor Standards Act prohibited child labor in interstate commerce and fixed a forty-cents-per-hour minimum wage and a forty-hour maximum work week. But so many exceptions to its provisions were made by Southern Congressmen who feared disruption of the South's cheap labor supply that millions of Americans were exempted from its provisions. Yet, weak though it was, the new law did secure wage raises for twelve million workers in industries involved in interstate commerce and provided a firm foundation upon which later Congresses could build.

But the bitterly fought labor act was to be the last New Deal reform that FDR was able to push through Congress. By 1939 the coalition against him had grown too strong. And, too, the recession of 1938 did not last very long. By midsummer, the economy began to climb again, if not speedily, steadily, and as conditions improved, once again public support for reform waned.

But the lessening of public enthusiasm for the New Deal in 1938 and 1939 had other grounds than just returning prosperity. For seven years Americans had given enthusiastic support to a vigorous and adventurous effort to rebuild the American way of life. They were tired. More than that they were discouraged. Ten years after the Crash there were still eight million unemployed. Many people were beginning to believe that massive unemployment would remain a permanent feature of American society. Even New Deal supporters like New York's progressive and rambunctious Mayor Fiorello LaGuardia felt that "instead of considering the situation as an emergency, we accept the inevitable, that we are now in a new normal." Harry Hopkins wrote that America had become "bored with the poor, the unemployed and the insecure."

During the midterm elections of 1938, Roosevelt determined to carry the battle to his conservative Democratic opponents on their home grounds. He toured the country speaking out for New Dealers and condemning Democrats who opposed his programs. But here FDR ran into the hard fact that Senators and Representatives were all but immune to this kind of attack in their personal political citadels. Roosevelt's tour could not be proved to have helped New Dealers who won, and was a disaster as far as trying to unseat conservatives. Furthermore, the Republicans, profiting by both public weariness and Democratic dissension, picked up eighty-one seats in the House of Representatives and eight in the Senate. There was still a comfortable Democratic majority in both houses, but now, more than ever, FDR had to rely on the sometime support of Democratic conservatives. The new Congress became not a battlefield for new social legislation, but a rear guard action to preserve what gains the New Deal had made. Conservatives attempted to amend the Wagner Labor Relations Act, to dismantle the Social Security program, and to do away with AAA. They launched blistering personal attacks on Roosevelt administrators such as Harry Hopkins. And if New Deal supporters in Congress could still muster enough strength to beat back these attacks, they could make no advances. From the fall of 1938 on, the New Deal was to remain at stalemate.

American public interest in reform not only diminished through weariness and disappointment. It was also distracted by the gathering drum taps of approaching war. From the very beginning of Roosevelt's first administration, the steady tapping of that distant drum had been audible. Just one day after Roosevelt entered the White House, on March 5, 1933, Adolf Hitler had won supreme power in Germany. At first, the menace of European Fascism was but dimly understood by Americans. Many, especially the older Wilsonian liberals, felt that American entrance into World War I had wrecked the hopes of reform, subverted American ideals, and led to the arch conservatism of the twenties. Furthermore, the collapse of American idealism in 1919 and 1920 had been accompanied by sour revelations of munitions industry influence in international affairs and by a harsh awakening to the fact that European powers had fought the war primarily for motives of greed. Millions of men, it appeared, had died not only in vain, but unwittingly on the ugly altars of colonialism, rival imperialisms, and blind stupidity. Americans wanted no more of that. Nor did they want, as the election of 1920 demonstrated, any entanglements whatsoever with foreign powers, even in the League of Nations.

Roosevelt, by background, inclination, and conviction, was an internationalist. He had fought hard for the League of Nations and had advocated lower tariffs. But the realities of political life were such that by the time he ran for the Presidency in 1932, FDR felt obliged to recant his support for the League and, under the prodding of economic nationalists such as Raymond Moley and Rexford Tugwell, to retreat from lowering tariffs. His early policy (and New Deal conviction) that the causes of depression were national, not international, led to American wrecking of the London Economic Conference of 1933. Despite this, Secretary of State Cordell Hull remained firmly wedded to the internationalist conviction and kept arguing for reciprocal trade treaties. The idea behind this was that the President should be freed from political pressures and private lobby interests in deciding questions of international trade. Congress should, for specified periods of time, allow the President to negotiate freely with foreign governments to lower tariff barriers on a reciprocal basis. Hull won over to his viewpoint Henry Wallace and other New Dealers as well as Republican internationalists like Henry Stimson—and he finally won over FDR. Accordingly, in June, 1934, Congress passed the Trade Agreements Act which permitted the President to raise or lower tariff rates as much as 50 per cent with nations which would reciprocate with similar concessions for American goods. By 1938 Cordell Hull had negotiated eighteen such treaties.

It was the pressing need for foreign trade during the Depression years, as well as growing political maturity, which led also to the recognition and establishment of diplomatic relations with Soviet Russia. While such bodies as the Daughters of the American Revolution violently opposed recognition, businessmen joined liberals in backing the measure. Maxim Litvinoff, representing the Soviet Union, arrived in Washington on November 7, 1933, to begin negotiations. A few weeks later, his mission a success, Litvinoff sailed home after a farewell dinner at the Waldorf Astoria Hotel in New York at which he was feted by representatives of the House of Morgan, the Pennsylvania Railroad, and the Chase National Bank, among other firms thirsty for Russian trade.

American relations with Central and South America, so long left in the hands of the United Fruit Company, imperialistic rabble-rousers such as William Randolph Hearst, and the United States Marines, were also to undergo a dramatic change at the hands of FDR and Cordell Hull. FDR had proclaimed that American relations with South American countries should be those of a "good neighbor," and as early as December, 1933, he had publicly renounced the use of armed force by the United States in her relations with sister nations of the Western Hemisphere. In the spring of 1934, the United States and Cuba agreed to end American control of Cuban finances, and the United States Marines finally left Haiti. Furthermore, when, in 1938, the Mexican government expropriated foreign oil and silver interests, FDR refused to rush in American troops to protect American investments. He had appointed his liberal mentor of World War I days, Josephus Daniels, as American Ambassador to Mexico, and that stoutly progressive old gentleman sympathized much more with Mexican reformers than with American oil companies.

But despite the New Deal's Good Neighbor Policy in Latin America, neither the Congress nor the American people were prepared to support a positive program which would contain European Fascism. Most Americans were too busy with their own dreadful problems to pay much attention to events in distant Europe. Although Hitler's policy of persecuting the Jews drew widespread condemnation in the United States, very few Americans were willing to even impose an economic embargo against Germany, much less any measures which might, however remotely, smack of war. To make sure that America would never again be dragged into what isolationists viewed as Europe's sordid affairs, Congress, over Roosevelt's objections, passed in 1935 a Neutrality Act which forbade shipment of arms to nations at war and the transport of arms on American ships to belligerents, and even empowered the President to withdraw the protection of the United States from American citizens traveling on the vessels of belligerent nations.

The Neutrality Act, and the spirit which supported it, became an agony not only for FDR and the New Deal, but also for an increasing segment of the American people who foresaw disaster ahead. When Italy invaded Ethiopia in 1935, the Neutrality Act prevented any help to Ethiopia; when Spanish Fascists rebelled against Spain's republican government and embarked on the long and bloody Spanish Civil War, the Neutrality Act, applied with fine impartiality to the rebel forces and the legal government of Spain alike, worked entirely against the republicans. When Japan invaded China in 1937, it was again the Neutrality Act which prevented American aid to China.

On the other hand, the Neutrality Act made no provision for the stoppage of shipments of such fundamental supplies as oil to belligerents, or of scrap iron. And because Italy, Japan, and the Nazi-Fascist supporters of the Spanish rebels controlled the seas in their war zones, American oil, scrap iron, and other raw materials flowed freely to the enemies of democracy. Any attempt to stop such shipments was assailed in Congress and the press as a direct blow at much needed foreign trade. So aware were Congressmen of the profits American business was missing that in 1937 they amended the Neutrality Act to permit belligerent nations to buy arms in the United States, but only if they paid cash money and carted the weapons away in their own vessels. Evidently isolationists liked profits as much as anyone else, provided "business as usual" could be maintained.

But business as usual could be maintained less and less as the thirties went on. Hitler's obvious intention to conquer Europe and perhaps the world, the ravings of Mussolini, and Japan's poorly disguised ambitions were awakening more and more Americans to the dangers ahead. In 1937, FDR made a speech in Chicago in which he called for an international "quarantine" of aggressors; a majority (however slim) of Americans supported him. But when it came to defining just what was meant by "quarantine," FDR hedged. "It is a terrible thing," the President later recalled, "to look over your shoulder when you are trying to lead—and to find no one there." Even when, in December, 1937, the Japanese carefully, and purposefully, bombed and sank the American gunboat *Panay* lying at anchor on China's Yangtse River, isolationist sentiment was so strong that what might have provoked an earlier administration (such as the McKinley administration of 1898) to war was passed over when apologies and cash reparations were received from Tokyo.

1938—a year of recession, and the drum beat was louder. It was heard now right at home. Organizations such as William Dudley Pelley's Silver Shirts (SS) attracted thousands of members with a program of frank Fascism and anti-semitism. Father Coughlin, back again in politics despite his promise of 1936, had organized the Christian Front as a Jew-baiting Fascist group whose members held rifle target practice weekly at their camp in New Jersey. Fritz Kuhn's German-American Bund was able to attract 20,000 people to its Hitlerian revels in Madison Square Garden. That was the year in which Hitler, having digested Austria, swallowed part of Czechoslovakia, the year of the shameful Munich Pact which brought England and France to the final depths of appeasement.

And it was in 1938, too, that Roosevelt asked Congress for a starting appropriation of $300 million for defense, while English and French orders for munitions, planes, guns, and tanks began to descend on American industry. Gradually the big steel companies expanded their production, aircraft manufacturers began to plan for new plants. There was a demand for American food as Europe began feverishly to stockpile against inevitable war, and, amazingly to a generation which had all but lost the memory of prosperity, the "HELP WANTED" signs began to go up on factories across the nation. Despite the fact that until 1941 six million Americans (of whom half were Negroes) were to remain unemployed, the onset of war marked the end of the Great Depression. By the end of 1938 few Americans doubted that prosperity was, at last, really just around the corner. The New Deal was ended not only by conservative Congressional opposition but also by the fact that it seemed less and less necessary. As prosperity returned, political argument centered more and more on whether or not and to what extent the United States should involve itself in the fight against Fascism. When war broke out in Europe in September, 1939, domestic concerns were overshadowed not only by questions of national survival, but also by the fact that many domestic problems were being automatically solved as the nation rearmed. The Presidential campaign of 1940, fought between FDR and ex-Commonwealth and Southern TVA foe Wendell Willkie ("a simple, barefoot, Wall Street lawyer," Ickes called him), was to be waged primarily as a debate on foreign affairs, and FDR's re-election was brought about as much by reluctance to lose his leadership while war clouds gathered, as by support of New Deal domestic policies. The New Deal had not, finally, solved the problem of depression—war and preparation for war accomplished that. But as the pall of eleven years of depression lifted from the land, there were few sounds of public rejoicing. All that could be heard as the Depression ended was the summons of the steady drummer; a continuous rolling of the drum now, ever louder, ever nearer.

epilogue The Fervent Years

I think the true discovery of America is before us. I
think the true fulfillment of our spirit, of our people,
of our mighty and immortal land, is yet to come. I think
the true discovery of our own democracy is still before us.
                                        Thomas Wolfe

Hunger and hurt are the great begetters of brotherhood:
Humiliation has gotten much love:
Danger I say is the nobler father and mother.

.   .   .   .

Brotherhood! No word said can make you brothers!
Brotherhood only the brave earn and by danger or
Harm or by bearing hurt and by no other.
                                        Archibald MacLeish

JUST AS no one believed it when it came, so no one really believed
it was over. Oh, there was war prosperity, all right; what else
could you expect with 15 million men in uniform and factories
turning out military planes every minute on the minute and liberty ships steaming across the oceans bearing billions of tons of
food and munitions and hardware, all of which was to be con-
sumed, blown up, sunk, or simply thrown away? But it could
not last, of course. When the war ended, what then? Then there

would be the same old problems of overproduction, of millions of men for whom no work could be found. War was a very efficient disposer of surplus goods and surplus people. But despite the dreams of some of the more militant among Americans, war could not go on forever. Eventually victory, unfortunately, had to come. And with victory, peace. And with peace, depression. It had been so in 1919 and it would be so in 1946.

But it didn't quite happen that way. There was a mild recession which lasted but a few months in 1946 and 1947, and then the American economy began to expand rapidly. It has, with two recessions (neither of which would have been honored by that name during the years of the Great Depression), been expanding ever since. At first men could not really believe it; they kept their fingers crossed. When Henry Wallace, making a forlorn bid for the Presidency in 1948, published a book entitled *Henry Wallace and Sixty Million Jobs*, most people jeered. Sixty million jobs would never be available in America, even during prosperous times. Today, of course, there are close to 80 million people steadily employed in the United States.

Gradually people began to believe it. They began to believe that not only was the Depression over, but that it would never happen that way again. And a new generation grew up who knew nothing of depression. All they could see of it was the quiet anxiety that seemed to flicker permanently in their parents' eyes; the overwhelming desire for "security" at almost any price displayed by those who had known the thirties. And gradually, people became willing to face the old pain, to ask: How did it happen? Can it happen again?

No one is yet certain of the precise reasons why the Great Depression came to America. It was not directly caused by the Wall Street Crash—there had been other financial collapses before 1929 quite as severe as that, and although they had sometimes (not always) been followed by periods of depression, they had never led to ten years of it. No one was even precisely sure why the Crash itself occurred. But *probably* . . .

Probably the Crash was caused by speculation in an uncontrolled and unregulated securities market. Probably hysteria and simple greed led to a wild overinflation of stock values in 1929, just as they had during many a false boom and bust in preceding years and centuries. Probably the speculation was more severe and widespread because in 1929, for the first time in history, people were exposed to the application of modern advertising techniques in the selling of stock and the inflating of values. Probably, as with all hysterias and speculations, it was basically a question of confidence. When the largest investors, who knew better than anyone just how inflated values were and upon what shaky grounds the pyramid of speculation had been built, began to sell, confidence evaporated and a great rush of selling destroyed the market —a chain-reaction effect which snowballed.

Could that happen again? Not in quite the same way. The stock market, because of New Deal legislation, is fairly well controlled today. The Federal Reserve Board has the right to fix higher interest rates on its loans; the Securities Exchange Commission has the right to require higher margin rates or, if necessary, 100 per cent payment for stocks. And the activities of the Exchange itself, and of its governors and the brokers who serve it, are now hedged around with all sorts of restrictions and controls. But there is nothing to prevent foolishness. Another generation of Americans could again indulge in an orgy of stock speculation, thereby inflating values and leading to an eventual bust. It has happened time and again throughout history. It probably will not happen while there are still enough people around who remember 1929. But such people grow fewer with the passing years. The glittering dream of something for nothing dies hard in the human breast; it will, no doubt, one day manifest itself again and, inevitably, lead to stock collapse.

If speculation and lack of controls produced the panic of 1929, what produced the Great Depression, an event unique in American history? There are as many answers as there are economists, sociologists, and historians who investigate the problem. One is probably the overproduction caused by technical progress, combined with the fact that money earned by technical advances was withheld from labor through abysmally low wages and from the public through continuing high prices. People produced a tremendous amount of goods but did not receive, in wages, the money necessary to buy those goods. Furthermore, the structure of the economy, controlled by a very few large corporations, saddled with holding companies and riddled with dishonesty, was so rigid, unyielding, and fragile that a severe blow to one part of it brought the entire structure toppling down. That severe blow, probably, was the 1929 Crash. But without the inherent weakness of the economy, the Crash would not have brought such severe and prolonged disaster.

Could it happen again? Given, say, another crash, or perhaps the obliteration of America's foreign markets, or some other such blow, could another Great Depression settle over the land? Again the answer is, not in the same way, if at all. The strength of American labor unions assures that increases in productivity are matched (and now sometimes overmatched) by increases in pay and purchasing power. Such government programs as the Social Security Law and unemployment insurance acts ensure that most Americans, no matter what happens to private industry, will continue to receive at least subsistence money from their government. Bank failures are all but impossible, because of the Federal Deposit Insurance Act and other governmental controls. In other words, if somehow the American economy should again be laid low, the impact of the disaster upon ordinary people would be much less in absolute terms. *But not in relative terms.*

For, thirty-five years after the Depression, Americans had become used to an incredibly high standard of living. It was a standard which no amount of government assistance in times of crisis could possibly replace. To fall from a high place hurts more than to fall from a low place. It is perhaps more than just probable that should another depression hit the United States, it would spell the end of the capitalistic economic system.

If the causes of the Crash and the Great Depression can be identified only with the word *probable*, what brought it to an end? The immediate answer, of course, is World War II. But after the war, why didn't the depression return? Largely because American industry found itself almost alone in being unscathed in a world desperately in need of goods. Whole continents had to be rebuilt, and only American industry could provide the tools and products with which to accomplish the task. Furthermore, because of the manpower shortage of the war years and the accumulating power of labor unions, a huge reservoir of purchasing strength had been built up at home, with nothing to spend it on. After four years of war (and a decade of depression) Americans needed everything—and they had the money to buy it. On the other hand, the foreign market had no money with which to buy. That, however, was speedily fixed up by the American government giving and lending many billions of dollars abroad. In other words, the federal government took money from American pockets in the form of taxes to lend to empty foreign pockets so that the money could eventually be paid back to American industry and, partly, to American workers. A happy circle, arranged and financed by the federal government. Nor was it given grudgingly by the American people, who, for humanitarian and practical political reasons, would not permit a world to starve. Whatever sacrifices Americans may have made (and they have been comparatively slight) to rebuild and support a war-shattered world have been more than amply repaid in continuing prosperity at home and at least some relative security abroad.

The New Deal did not, as has been pointed out, end the Depression. But it laid the foundation for whatever economic and social security Americans enjoy today. Subsequent Congresses, subsequent administrations have continued to build on these foundations. Without arguing the question of just how close the United States was to revolution from 1930 to 1934, it may be said that the New Deal probably saved the capitalistic system in America. Roosevelt's entire program was based on the idea that a just society could be built by imposing a welfare state on capitalistic foundations. The foundations themselves—the complex system of private profit, private ownership, and all the public *mores* in which they were entangled—were not attacked, or even seriously questioned. New Deal reforms were just that—reforms, not revolutionary measures.

The New Deal answer to the depressed end of the business cycle—the pumping of huge sums of federal tax money into the economy in the form of public works and relief programs—did not bring about recovery. But, given the ground rules of capitalism, it was nevertheless the correct answer. Despite the outcries of the conservatives, the New Deal simply did not spend *enough* money! Neither Roosevelt nor any of his advisors could imagine the vast sums which would be required to regenerate prosperity. Although, in 1938, the President won a $3.7 billion appropriation from Congress for public spending, it was soon to be demonstrated that only the expenditure of $50 billion per year (in war purchases and, later, in overseas aid and relief) could effect basic support for the economy. And, in fact, today the United States Government, directly and indirectly, spends closer to $75 billion a year in the American economy. And few complain—but some wonder. They wonder what would happen to the economy if, say, the more than $50 billion per year spent for military preparedness and war were suddenly to come to an end.

The New Deal reached stalemate in 1938 and was drowned by the war. Unfortunately, also drowned was the spirit which had supported it. The years following World War II were to see a dreary repetition of the hysteria, public apathy, and return to overweening private greed which marked the years after World War I. There was to be another and even more damaging "Red scare" presided over by Wisconsin's Senator Joe McCarthy (and supported by a large segment of the American people). There was to be a return to business ethics and private morality in place of the public ethics of the thirties. Bruce Barton's revelation of Christ as a businessman was hardly more indicative of the spirit of the twenties than General Motors President Charles Wilson's brusque "What's-good-for-General-Motors-is-good-for-America" was of the fifties. While the new-found prosperity of America was poured into goods, services, and hardware, into ever bigger and more vulgar automobiles, ever flashier kitchens, ever more clever gadgets, it was to be withheld from the public sector of the economy. The shiny new cars cluttered poorly paved city streets. The flashy kitchens were often found in crumbling public housing. Well-dressed children attended public schools whose buildings were a national disgrace; they were taught by teachers whose salaries were a national shame. And, once again, as in the twenties, voices of protest against the decay of the public community were attacked as "subversive," or "un-American."

And the New Deal left much unfinished business behind. There remained that one third of a nation ill-housed (now probably one half of a nation); that one third of a nation ill-fed (thousands of people were shown to be starving to death in the South in 1967). And, for all its good wishes, the New Deal had done little to win for Negroes their rightful place in American society. All these problems, and many more, remained to haunt the American landscape in later years. Basic to all of them remained the problem central to the New Deal itself. Can a society based on free enterprise—whose citizens are raised from the cradle to believe in competition as the basis of life, and the success of the individual (at no matter what private or public cost) in that competition as the ultimate good—provide a just, inspiring, secure, or even sane framework for the human body, mind, and spirit? And if not, what kind of society could possibly take its place? Certainly not a regimented one, or one in which the worship of success is replaced by the worship of the state (or of any state dogma, philosophy, or public religion). One of the great accomplishments of the New Deal was to keep the future open to answer this question. No foreclosures took place in America as they did in some foreign lands. Neither Fascism nor Communism nor any variants thereon were substituted for honest and energetic experimentation, questioning, and exploration. So long as the future *remains* open there is reason to hope that problems— slowly, painfully perhaps, but progressively—*can* be solved. But only great determination, deep devotion, and a willingness towards commitment can provide that public passion upon which the American experiment has always been based.

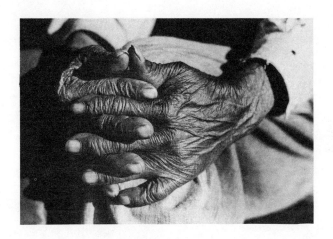

Bibliography

A Suggested Reading List will be found at the end of the Bibliography

AARON, DANIEL, *Writers on the Left* (Garden City, N. Y., 1961).

ABBOTT, GRACE, *From Relief to Social Security* (Chicago, 1940).

ALBERTSON, DEAN, *Roosevelt's Farmer* (New York, 1961).

ALSOP, JOSEPH, AND CATLEDGE, TURNER, *The 168 Days* (Garden City, N. Y., 1938).

———, AND KINTNER, ROBERT, *American White Paper* (New York, 1940).

ARMSTRONG, LOUISE, *We Too Are the People* (Boston, 1938).

ARNOLD, THURMAN, *The Folklore of Capitalism* (New Haven, Conn., 1937).

BAKKE, E. WRIGHT, *Citizens Without Work* (New Haven, Conn., 1940).

BEARD, CHARLES AND MARY, *America in Midpassage* (2 vols.) (New York, 1939).

BENEDICT, MURRAY, *Farm Policies of the United States, 1790–1950* (New York, 1953).

BERNSTEIN, IRVING, *The Lean Years* (Boston, 1960).

BLUM, JOHN M., *From the Morgenthau Diaries* (Boston, 1959).

BROOKS, ROBERT R., *As Steel Goes . . .* (New Haven, Conn., 1940).

BURNS, JAMES M., *Roosevelt: The Lion and the Fox* (New York, 1956).

CLURMAN, HAROLD, *The Fervent Years* (New York, 1957).

CONKIN, PAUL, *Tomorrow a New World* (Ithaca, N. Y., 1959).

COOKE, ALISTAIR, *A Generation on Trial* (New York, 1950).

CRAWFORD, ARTHUR W., *Monetary Management Under the New Deal* (Washington, 1940).

CREEL, GEORGE, *Rebel at Large* (New York, 1947).

DAVIS, FORREST, *Huey Long* (New York, 1935).

DEGLER, CARL, *Out of Our Past* (New York, 1959).

DERBER, MILTON, AND YOUNG, EDWIN, *Labor and the New Deal* (Madison, Wis., 1957).

DORFMAN, JOSEPH, *The Economic Mind in American Civilization* (New York, 1959).

DRUMMOND, DONALD, *The Passing of American Neutrality, 1937–1941* (Ann Arbor, Mich., 1955).

ECCLES, MARRINER, *Beckoning Frontiers* (New York, 1951).

EINAUDI, MARIO, *The Roosevelt Revolution* (New York, 1959).

FARLEY, JAMES A., *Jim Farley's Story* (New York, 1948).

FEDERAL WRITERS' PROJECT, *These Are Our Lives* (Chapel Hill, N. C., 1939).

FLANAGAN, HALLIE, *Arena* (New York, 1940).

FREIDEL, FRANK, *Franklin D. Roosevelt* (3 vols.) (Boston, 1952–56).

GALBRAITH, JOHN K., *The Great Crash* (Boston, 1955).

GEISMAR, MAXWELL, *Writers in Crisis* (Boston, 1942).

GINZBERG, ELI, *The Unemployed* (New York, 1943).

GOLDMAN, ERIC, *Rendezvous With Destiny* (New York, 1952).

GUNTHER, JOHN, *Roosevelt in Retrospect* (New York, 1950).

GURKO, LEO, *The Angry Decade* (New York, 1947).

HARRIS, HERBERT, *American Labor* (New Haven, Conn., 1938).

HENDEL, SAMUEL, *Charles Evans Hughes and the Supreme Court* (New York, 1951).

HOLLAND, KENNETH, AND HILL, FRANK E., *Youth in the CCC* (Washington, 1942).

HOPKINS, HARRY, *Spending to Save* (New York, 1936).

HOWARD, DONALD, *The WPA and Federal Relief Policy* (New York, 1943).

HOWE, IRVING, AND COSER, LEWIS, *The American Communist Party* (Boston, 1957).

ICKES, HAROLD, *The Autobiography of a Curmudgeon* (New York, 1948).

——, *The Secret Diaries of Harold Ickes* (3 vols.) (New York, 1954).

Jackson, Robert, *The Struggle for Judicial Supremacy* (New York, 1941).

Johnson, Gen. Hugh, *The Blue Eagle from Egg to Earth* (Garden City, N. Y., 1935).

Johnson, Walter, *1600 Pennsylvania Avenue* (Boston, 1960).

———, *William Allen White's America* (New York, 1947).

Joslin, Theodore, *Hoover Off the Record* (Garden City, N. Y., 1934).

Kane, Harnett, *Louisiana Hayride* (New York, 1941).

Kempton, Murray, *Part of Our Time* (New York, 1955).

Komarovsky, Mirra, *The Unemployed Man and His Family* (New York, 1940).

Kraus, Henry, *The Many and the Few* (Los Angeles, 1947).

Lee, Alfred M. and Elizabeth B., *The Fine Art of Propaganda* (New York, 1939).

Lens, Sidney, *Left, Right and Center* (Hinsdale, Ill., 1949).

Lerner, Max, *Ideas for the Ice Age* (New York, 1941).

Lilienthal, David, *TVA: Democracy on the March* (New York, 1944).

Lindley, Betty and Ernest K., *A New Deal for Youth* (New York, 1939).

Lord, Russell, *The Wallaces of Iowa* (Boston, 1947).

Lowenthal, Leo, and Guterman, Norbert, *Prophets of Deceit* (New York, 1949).

Lubell, Samuel, *The Future of American Politics* (New York, 1951).

Lynd, Robert and Helen, *Middletown in Transition* (New York, 1937).

Meriam, Lewis, *Relief and Social Security* (Washington, 1946).

McConnell, Grant, *The Decline of Agrarian Democracy* (Berkeley, Calif., 1953).

McCoy, Donald, *Angry Voices* (Lawrence, Kans., 1958).

McKenney, Ruth, *Industrial Valley* (New York, 1939).

Mitchell, Broadus, *Depression Decade* (New York, 1947).

Moley, Raymond, *After Seven Years* (New York, 1939).

Myrdal, Gunnar, *An American Dilemma* (New York, 1944).

Perkins, Frances, *The Roosevelt I Knew* (New York, 1946).

Phillips, Harlan, *Felix Frankfurter Reminisces* (New York, 1960).

Richberg, Donald, *The Rainbow* (New York, 1936).

ROLLINS, ALFRED, *Roosevelt and Howe* (New York, 1962).

ROOSE, KENNETH, *The Economics of Recession and Revival* (New Haven, Conn., 1954).

ROOSEVELT, ELEANOR, *This I Remember* (New York, 1949).

ROOSEVELT, ELLIOT, *FDR: His Personal Letters, 1928–1945* (2 vols.) (New York, 1950).

ROOSEVELT, JAMES, AND SHALETT, SIDNEY, *Affectionately, F.D.R.* (New York, 1959).

ROSENMAN, SAMUEL, *The Public Papers and Addresses of Franklin D. Roosevelt* (13 vols.) (New York, 1938–50).

————, *Working With Roosevelt* (New York, 1952).

SCHLESINGER, ARTHUR M., JR., *The Age of Roosevelt* (3 vols.) (Boston, 1957–60).

SELDES, GILBERT, *The Years of the Locust* (Boston, 1933).

SHERWOOD, ROBERT E., *Roosevelt and Hopkins* (New York, 1962).

TUGWELL, REXFORD G., *The Battle for Democracy* (New York, 1935).

————, *The Democratic Roosevelt* (Garden City, N.Y., 1957).

TULLY, GRACE, *F.D.R., My Boss* (New York, 1949).

WALLACE, HENRY, *New Frontiers* (New York, 1934).

WARREN, HARRIS, *Herbert Hoover and the Great Depression* (New York, 1959).

WECHSLER, JAMES, *The Age of Suspicion* (New York, 1953).

————, *Labor Baron* (New York, 1944).

WECTER, DIXON, *The Age of the Great Depression, 1929–1941* (New York, 1948).

WOLFSKILL, GEORGE, *The Revolt of /the Conservatives* (Boston, 1962).

Suggested Reading:

BERNSTEIN, IRVING, *The Lean Years* (Boston, 1960). Labor's battles before the New Deal.

FEDERAL WRITERS' PROJECT, *These Are Our Lives* (Chapel Hill, N.C., 1939). Telling it as it *really* was, on the personal level.

FREIDEL, FRANK, *Franklin D. Roosevelt* (Boston, 1952–56). Magisterial but as yet incomplete biography of FDR.

GALBRAITH, JOHN K., *The Great Crash* (Boston, 1955). The most enlightening, and certainly the wittiest, book on Wall Street's sorriest days.

JOHNSON, WALTER, *William Allen White's America* (New York, 1947). A salty Republican but not unsympathetic view of the decade.

PERKINS, FRANCES, *The Roosevelt I Knew* (New York, 1946). The best of all the personal reminiscences of FDR.

ROOSEVELT, ELEANOR, *This I Remember* (New York, 1949). What it was like to be a Roosevelt, by one of the greatest of them.

SCHLESINGER, ARTHUR M., JR., *The Age of Roosevelt* (Boston, 1957–60). What promises to be the definitive history of the era, as yet incomplete.

SHERWOOD, ROBERT E., *Roosevelt and Hopkins* (New York, 1962). Colorful biography of a team with a mission.

SWADOS, HARVEY (ed.), *The American Writer and the Great Depression* (New York, 1966). A brilliant discussion and compendium of the best in Depression fiction, poetry, and reportage.

WILSON, EDMUND, *American Jitters* (New York, 1932). Penetrating views of American life during the worst days of the Depression.

Index

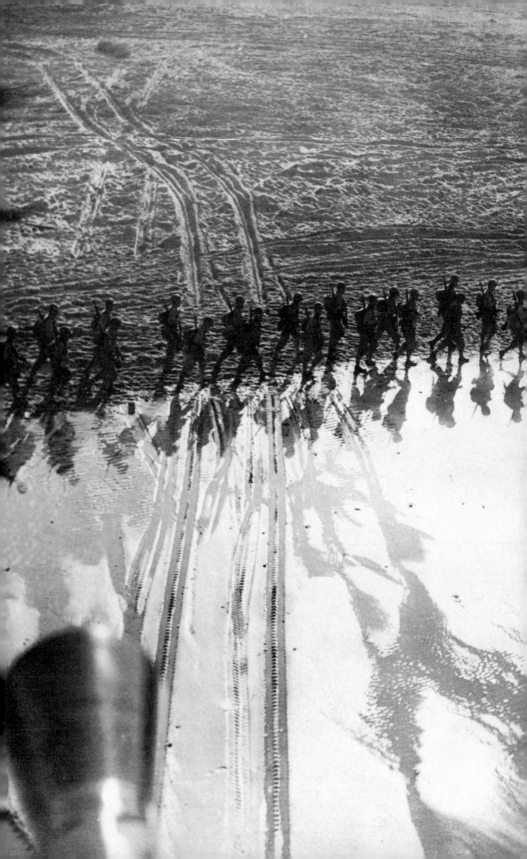